100

THE ROUGH GUIDE TO THE
BEST PLACES
ON EARTH 2020

100

THE ROUGH GUIDE TO THE
BEST PLACES
ON EARTH 2020

DISTRIBUTION

UK, Ireland and Europe
Apa Publications (UK) Ltd; sales@roughguides.com

United States and Canada
Ingram Publisher Services; ips@ingramcontent.com

Australia and New Zealand
Woodslane; info@woodslane.com.au

Southeast Asia
Apa Publications (SN) Pte; sales@roughguides.com

Worldwide
Apa Publications (UK) Ltd; sales@roughguides.com

SPECIAL SALES, CONTENT LICENSING AND CO-PUBLISHING

Rough Guides can be purchased in bulk quantities at discounted prices. We can create special editions, personalized jackets and corporate imprints tailored to your needs. sales@roughguides.com.
roughguides.com

Printed in China by RRD
All rights reserved
© 2019 Apa Digital (CH) AG
License edition © Apa Publications Ltd UK

1st Edition 2019

A catalogue record for this book is available from the British Library
ISBN: 978-1-78919-459-3
The publishers and authors have done their best to ensure the accuracy and currency of all the information in The Rough Guide to the 100 Best Places on Earth 2020, however, they can accept no responsibility for any loss, injury, or inconvenience sustained by any traveller as a result of information or advice contained in the guide.

HELP US UPDATE

We've gone to a lot of effort to ensure that the 1st edition of The Rough Guide to the 100 Best Places on Earth is accurate and up-to-date. But if you feel we've got it wrong or left something out, we'd like to know.
Please send your comments with the subject line "Rough Guide 100 Best Places Update" to mail@uk.roughguides.com. We'll credit all contributions and send a copy of the next edition (or any other Rough Guide if you prefer) for the very best emails.

THE ROUGH GUIDE TO THE
100 BEST PLACES ON EARTH
2020

Editor: Helen Fanthorpe

Managing editor: Carine Tracanelli

Picture editor: Aude Vauconsant

Cover photo research: Tom Smyth

Head of DTP and pre-press: Daniel May

Designer: Michal Ptasznik

Typesetter: Pradeep Thapliyal

Proofreader: Samantha Cook

100

THE ROUGH GUIDE TO THE BEST PLACES ON EARTH 2020

INTRODUCTION

Victoria Falls' thundering curtain of water crashing down along the border between Zambia and Zimbabwe; Lisbon's white cobbled streets, lined with colourful pot plants, snaking up the hillside; age-old temples at Bagan in Myanmar waking up in blood-orange light and shrouded in mist. These are the 100 Best Places on Earth 2020. Taking in exhilarating mountain scenery, dazzling cityscapes, pristine tropical islands, atmospheric ruins and sweeping savannahs, this book reaches every corner of the globe in the search for 2020's most spectacular spots.

Rough Guides' experienced team of authors and editors has been on the hunt for places that will be big news in 2020, as well as destinations that are unmissable, underrated, up-and-coming or back on the tourist map. And while whittling the world down to a round 100 was always going to be a hard task, we think our selection of emerging destinations for 2020 is pretty exciting.

Of the new places on the scene, we urge you to explore Ethiopia's remarkable collection of rock-cut churches, Tbilisi's glorious huddle of Art Nouveau buildings and candy-coloured facades, and the musical heritage of America's Deep South in Memphis and along the Tennessee Music Pathways. Iconic favourites like the Taj Mahal and the Grand Canyon, as well as unsung beauties like Cornwall and the Andaman Islands, complete the picture.

What follows is the ultimate bucket list.

ASIA

ANDAMAN ISLANDS

India's most remote region, the Andaman Islands are situated more than 100km off the east coast in the middle of the Bay of Bengal – only accessible via a domestic flight or a long ferry trip (three to five days) from the mainland. They're blessed with white sands, mangrove forests, palm trees and turquoise waters, and there's little to do here but relax in a hammock, eat a *thali* with fresh mango chutney and snorkel the coralfringed shorelines.

A long, thin cluster of approximately two hundred islands, the Andamans may be geographically closer to Thailand and Myanmar but they are unmistakeably Indian in culture, religion and cuisine. All but the most remote are populated in parts by indigenous tribes, and still see relatively few tourists.

Visitors arrive at Port Blair, once used as a gaol by the British Raj – the withering cells are now a tourist attraction – but most travellers quickly move on to the beaches of Havelock or its smaller neighbour, Neill. The outlying islands are richest in natural beauty, with the beaches of Smith and the coral around Cinque particularly dazzling.

Gorgonians in the Andaman Sea

Tourist boat heading to Neill Island

Port Blair prison

Vijaynagar Beach, Havelock Island

BAGAN

As the white heat of the day fades into dusk, around two thousand ancient Buddhist temples begin to glow a fiery red – just as they have every evening for hundreds of years. Bagan in Myanmar is unquestionably one of Asia's – indeed the world's – great sights. Its vast swathe of temples and pagodas rise from the hot, flat plains bordering the Ayeyarwady River, the landscape bristling with uncountable shrines and stupas which carpet the countryside in an almost surreal profusion and stretch as far as the eye can see.

Bagan's architecture comprises an extended variation on a few basic themes, with a handful of recurrent styles and structures that have gradually evolved over time; much of the pleasure of exploring its myriad temples is in unravelling the underlying motifs and meanings that underpin them.

Sulamani Temple

Buddha statues, Wat Pho

Market seller

Floating market

City panorama from Red Sky Bar

Wat Phra Kaeo and the Grand Palace

BANGKOK

Manic, thrilling, dynamic, exhausting, overpowering, titillating – the one thing Bangkok (Krung Thep in Thai; the "City of Angels") is not, is boring. However much time you spend here, you'll always find something to invigorate your senses, kick-start your enthusiasm and drive you crazy: frenetic markets and bustling temples, hip megamalls, zinging curries and cutting-edge clubs.

At first glance, this Asian supercity of 8.5 million people seems like a bewildering amalgam of new, old and indeterminate, all tossed together in a gigantic urban maze. It's hardly surprising that Bangkok should convey this impression, considering that only a little more than half a century ago much of what makes up the Thai capital was farmland. Bangkok began life as an amphibious city, and while its citizens may no longer live on the floating bamboo rafts of yesteryear, in among the chaotic jungle of modern Bangkok there remains a city fiercely proud of its past and its traditions.

Colourful prayer flags

BHUTAN

Hidden in the Himalayas, with all the matchless scenery you'd expect, the tiny country of Bhutan is staggeringly beautiful. Piercing peaks and plunging valleys fold into its borders, where you can climb to mountaintop monasteries, hike through ancient forests and horseback ride over lush green plains, while local guides give a real insight into the country's living spirituality.

Bhutan has been quietly forging its own path for centuries. Now, it's leading the way in sustainable tourism. With at least sixty percent forest cover, Bhutan takes environmental conservation seriously. It's already carbon negative, and is set to become the world's first fully organic nation by 2020, as well as limiting the number (and impact) of its tourists by imposing a per-day minimum spend for visitors.

Preservation is priceless, and travellers to this enchanting nation will leave with a real sense of what a privilege it is to experience Bhutan's natural, cultural and spiritual riches.

Rural village near Punakha

Red panda

Pack horses on the ascent to Bhonte La Pass

Taktsang Palphug Monastery

FORBIDDEN CITY

Lying at the heart of Beijing, the Forbidden City – or more accurately, the Imperial Palace – is among China's finest monuments. It is encased by a moat and, within the turreted walls, employs a wonderful symmetry and geomantic structure to achieve a balance between *yin* and *yang*: positive and negative energy. The city's spine is composed of eleven south-facing Halls or Gates, all colossal, exquisite and ornate. Branching off from this central vertebra are more than eight hundred buildings that share the exclusive combination of imperial colours: red walls and yellow roof tiles. Elsewhere, jade green, gold and azure blue decorate the woodwork, archways and balconies. The doors to the central halls are heavy, red, thick and studded with gold. All in all, the intricacy of the city's design is quite astonishing.

The central halls, impressive for demonstrating the sheer scale of imperial pomp, may be the most magnificent buildings, but for many visitors it's the side rooms, with their display of the more intimate accoutrements, that bring home the realities of court life for its inhabitants.

Intricate roof detail

Aerial view of the Forbidden City

Decorative doorway

Copper lion statue

GENGHIS KHAN EQUESTRIAN STATUE

The formidable Genghis Khan – or Chinggis Khaan as he's known locally – is the pride of the Mongolian people, his face plastered on everything from bank notes to cigarette packets and energy drinks. Rising out of the Mongolian steppe and circled by grazing animals and a few lonely *gers* (yurts), the Genghis Khan Equestrian Statue, 54km from the Mongolian capital of Ulaanbaatar, pays homage to the Mongol leader with a modern, man-made structure of titanic proportions.

This is the largest equestrian statue in the world – 44m tall and packing in some 250 tonnes of stainless steel – standing on a spot by the Tuul River where Genghis Khan is said to have found a golden whip. You can climb to the head of the horse for panoramas over the surrounding countryside, while the visitor centre contains an idiosyncratic museum with traditional Mongolian costumes and portraits of the Great Khans.

Genghis Khan Equestrian Statue and visitor centre

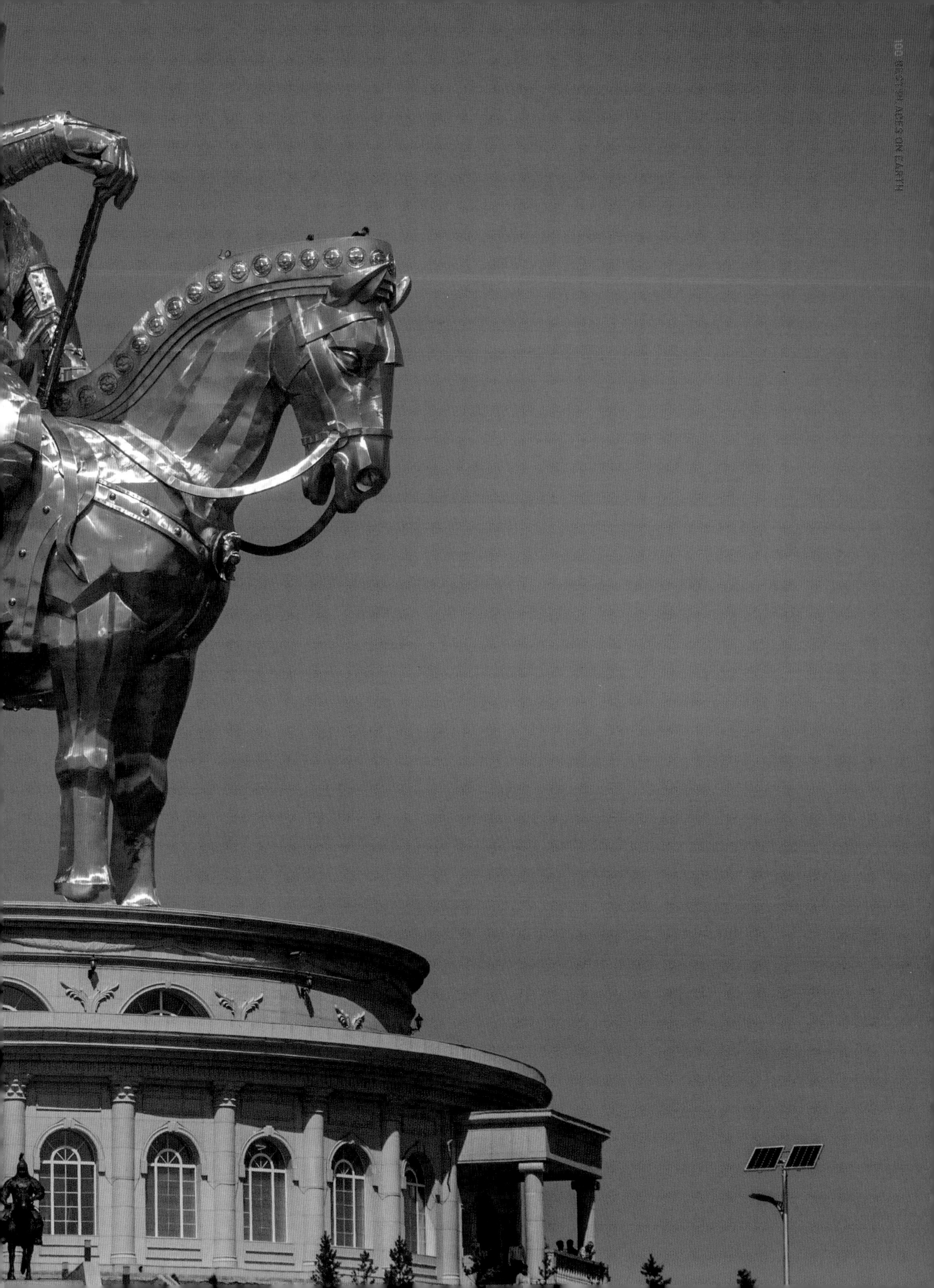

Jinshanling wall section

GREAT WALL OF CHINA

The practice of building walls along China's northern frontier began in the fifth century BC and continued until the sixteenth century, creating a discontinuous array of fortifications, which came to be known as *Wan Li Changcheng* – "the Great Wall" for English-speakers. Today, the line of the Wall can be followed from Shanhaiguan, by the Yellow Sea, to Jiayuguan in the northwestern deserts, a distance of around 3000km (or, according to a recent survey taking in all the disconnected sections, over 20,000km) – an astonishing feat of engineering.

As a symbol of national pride, the Wall's restored sections are besieged daily by tourists, while its image adorns all manner of products, from wine to cigarettes. Yet even the most visited section at Badaling is still easily one of China's most spectacular attractions. Mutianyu is somewhat less crowded, distant Simatai much less so, and far more beautiful. To see the wall in its crumbly glory, head out to Jinshanling, Jiankou or Huanghua, as yet largely untouched by development.

Statues around Juyong Pass

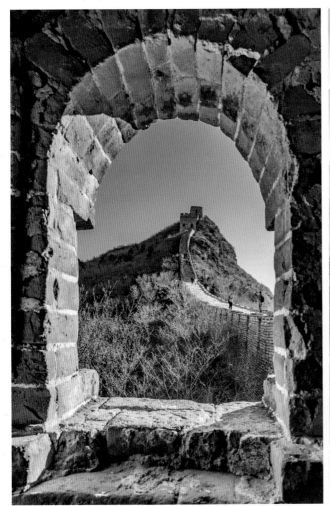

Stretch of wall between Gubeikou and Jinshanling

Great Wall at Jinshanling

Halong Bay from above

Traditional junks in Halong Bay

Thien Cung Cave

Monkey Island Beach

Inside a junk cabin

HALONG BAY

Cruising Halong Bay is on the bucket list of travellers the world over, and the magical landscape of northeast Vietnam doesn't disappoint.

The scattering of limestone pinnacles jutting out of the smooth waters is an incredible sight, and dropping anchor to explore small islands and caves is a once-in-a-lifetime experience. The best junk boats have private cabins and serve gourmet Vietnamese food – and in the early morning you can pull back the curtain to watch the sunlight dancing on the emerald green water. Try to avoid the rainy season, and if you haven't the budget to blow on a junk, then the ferry from Halong City (Tuan Chau Island) to Cat Ba Island reveals a glimpse of the majesty of Halong Bay at a fraction of the cost.

Scaling Mount Everest

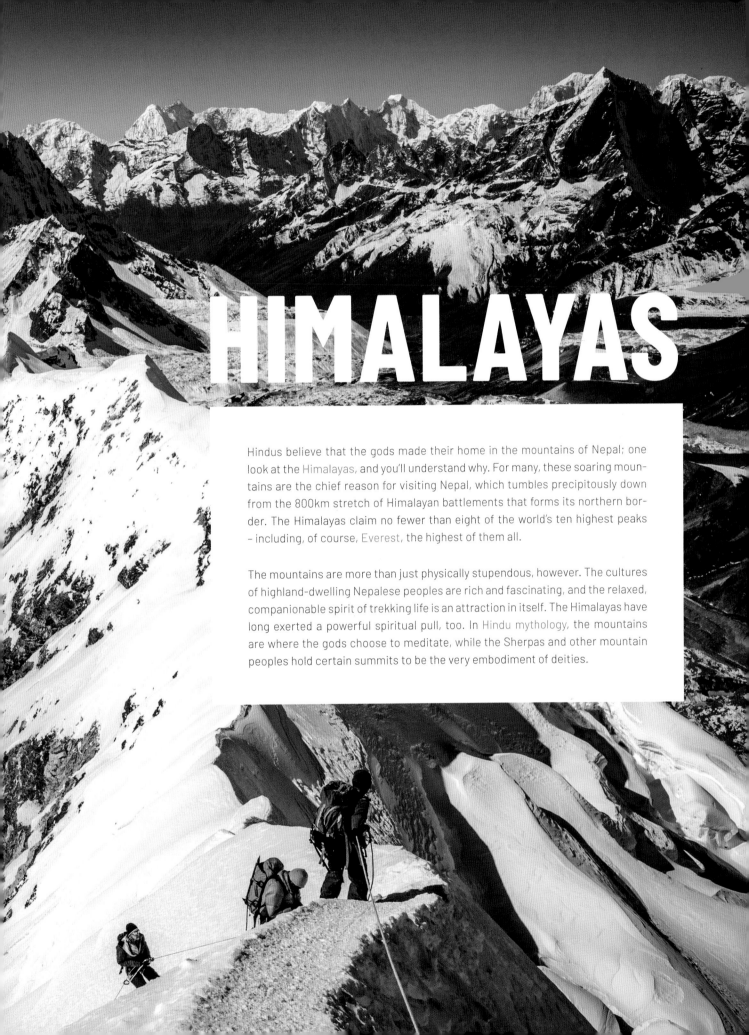

HIMALAYAS

Hindus believe that the gods made their home in the mountains of Nepal; one look at the Himalayas, and you'll understand why. For many, these soaring mountains are the chief reason for visiting Nepal, which tumbles precipitously down from the 800km stretch of Himalayan battlements that forms its northern border. The Himalayas claim no fewer than eight of the world's ten highest peaks – including, of course, Everest, the highest of them all.

The mountains are more than just physically stupendous, however. The cultures of highland-dwelling Nepalese peoples are rich and fascinating, and the relaxed, companionable spirit of trekking life is an attraction in itself. The Himalayas have long exerted a powerful spiritual pull, too. In Hindu mythology, the mountains are where the gods choose to meditate, while the Sherpas and other mountain peoples hold certain summits to be the very embodiment of deities.

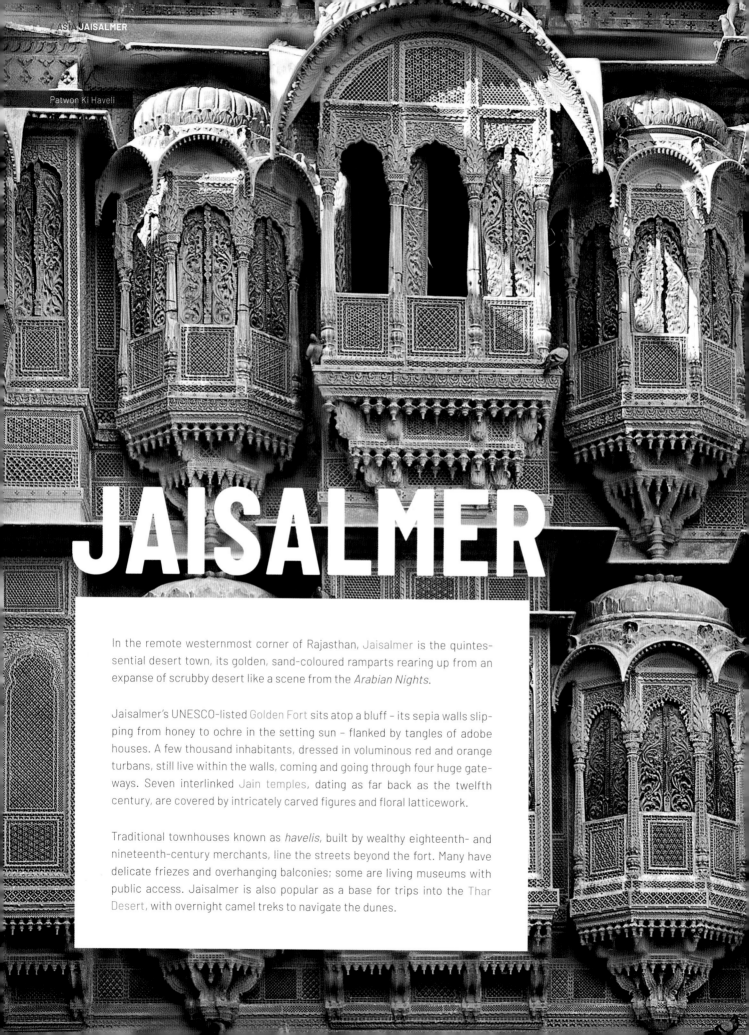

Patwon Ki Haveli

JAISALMER

In the remote westernmost corner of Rajasthan, Jaisalmer is the quintessential desert town, its golden, sand-coloured ramparts rearing up from an expanse of scrubby desert like a scene from the *Arabian Nights*.

Jaisalmer's UNESCO-listed Golden Fort sits atop a bluff – its sepia walls slipping from honey to ochre in the setting sun – flanked by tangles of adobe houses. A few thousand inhabitants, dressed in voluminous red and orange turbans, still live within the walls, coming and going through four huge gateways. Seven interlinked Jain temples, dating as far back as the twelfth century, are covered by intricately carved figures and floral latticework.

Traditional townhouses known as *havelis*, built by wealthy eighteenth- and nineteenth-century merchants, line the streets beyond the fort. Many have delicate friezes and overhanging balconies; some are living museums with public access. Jaisalmer is also popular as a base for trips into the Thar Desert, with overnight camel treks to navigate the dunes.

Golden Fort

Moustachioed Jaisalmer resident

Camel ride in the Thar Desert

Jain temple

Statue of Muhammad ibn Musa al-Khwarizmi

Pakhlavan Mahmoud's mausoleum

Weavers knotting a handmade carpet

Playing in the Islam Khoja complex

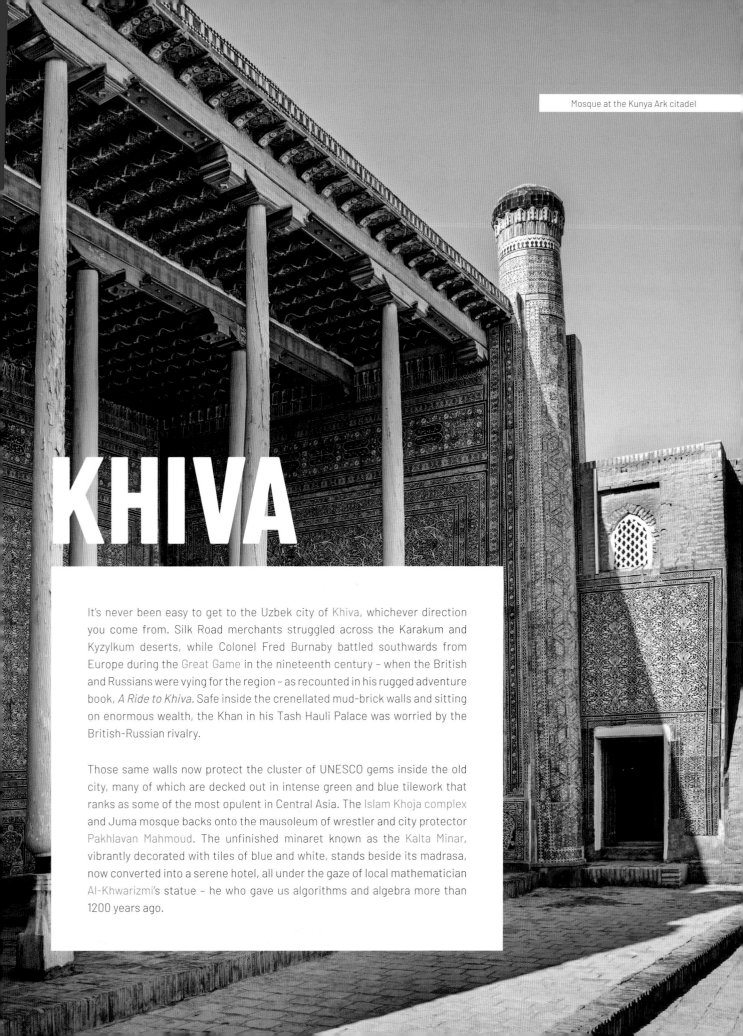

KHIVA

It's never been easy to get to the Uzbek city of Khiva, whichever direction you come from. Silk Road merchants struggled across the Karakum and Kyzylkum deserts, while Colonel Fred Burnaby battled southwards from Europe during the Great Game in the nineteenth century – when the British and Russians were vying for the region – as recounted in his rugged adventure book, *A Ride to Khiva*. Safe inside the crenellated mud-brick walls and sitting on enormous wealth, the Khan in his Tash Hauli Palace was worried by the British-Russian rivalry.

Those same walls now protect the cluster of UNESCO gems inside the old city, many of which are decked out in intense green and blue tilework that ranks as some of the most opulent in Central Asia. The Islam Khoja complex and Juma mosque backs onto the mausoleum of wrestler and city protector Pakhlavan Mahmoud. The unfinished minaret known as the Kalta Minar, vibrantly decorated with tiles of blue and white, stands beside its madrasa, now converted into a serene hotel, all under the gaze of local mathematician Al-Khwarizmi's statue – he who gave us algorithms and algebra more than 1200 years ago.

Typical Kyoto restaurant

Cherry blossom along the Philosopher's Path

Sunset at Kiyomizu temple

Pouring tea

KYOTO

The capital of Japan for more than a thousand years, Kyoto is endowed with an almost overwhelming legacy of ancient Buddhist temples, majestic palaces and gardens of every description, not to mention some of the country's most important works of art, its richest culture and most refined cuisine. For many people the very name Kyoto conjures up the classic image of Japan: streets of wooden houses, the click-clack of *geta* (traditional wooden sandals) on the paving stones and temple pagodas surrounded by cherry-blossom trees.

Kyoto's riches, however, are not at once obvious – leaving the station you're faced with what looks like a very normal Japanese cityscape, all concrete, commuters and convenience stores. But out of the centre, Kyoto's magic becomes palpable. You'll see lines of wooden teahouses, lush gardens where the moss is trimmed with tweezers, and white-faced *maiko* gliding down narrow streets in a scene straight from a woodblock print.

And this is before you've even begun to approach the city's big sights. Once you've viewed the autumn leaves along the Philosopher's Path, walked in dappled sunlight through the bamboo groves of Arashiyama, or gazed across the city from Kiyomizu temple, you'll understand why Kyoto is still the soul of Japan.

Arashiyama's bamboo groves

Chandratal lake, Spiti

LAHAUL AND SPITI

High in the mountains of northern India, in the arid and dramatic valleys of Lahaul and Spiti, adventurous souls trek to glaciers and snowfields to drink in wide-open vistas dotted with snow-topped chocolate-coloured mountains, remote villages and Buddhist *gompas* with prayer flags fluttering in the wind. Within the flick of a yak's tail of the border with Tibet, the region's traditional costume and Buddhism are a legacy of the Tibetan influence that has permeated the area from the east.

Until now, this remote region has largely been inaccessible to outsiders in the winter, when the Rohtang Pass on the Leh-Manali highway is blocked by snow or landslides for months at a time. However, in 2020, the high-altitude pass to Lahaul-Spiti will be replaced by the longest tunnel in India and this hauntingly beautiful frozen region will welcome trailblazing skiers and boarders to its slopes.

Infinity pool against the Indian Ocean

Scuba diving around Lhaviyani Atoll

Dinner on the beach

Fresh seafood

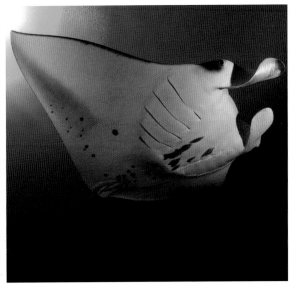
Manta ray

MALDIVES

In the balmy waters of the Indian Ocean, the chain of 26 atolls that makes up the Maldives is synonymous with white-powder beaches, picture-perfect palms and life being lived in the lap of luxury. For once, the tourist clichés are all true: nowhere else on earth will you find such blissful beaches, glassy waters and eye-watering extravagance. Accommodation extends into the ocean on stilts, staffed by Michelin-starred chefs and personal butlers; you'll also come across an infinity pool lit by twinkling stars, a beachside cinema, and underwater spaces – spas, restaurants, bedrooms and even a nightclub – surrounded by colourful tropical fish.

Marine life is abundant here, and the Maldives supports some of the world's best snorkelling and diving. Multi-coloured coral walls and deep caves sustain schools of pretty fish as well as some larger creatures of the deep: manta rays, whale sharks and hammerheads all call the islands their home.

NUSA TENGGARA

In Nusa Tenggara – the "islands of the southeast" – Indonesia's archipelagic nature comes to the fore. This string of small worlds stretching between Bali and East Timor is perfectly designed for island-hopping. Each landfall is strikingly distinct in landscape and culture – from lush, mountainous, Catholic-majority Flores to the scorched grasslands of Sumba, where traditions of ancestor worship still endure.

For years, poor infrastructure meant that Nusa Tenggara was the preserve of only the hardiest backpackers. But the transformation of Labuan Bajo – gateway to the neighbouring Komodo National Park, conveniently located midway along the chain at the western tip of Flores – from sleepy harbour village to well-connected and increasingly sophisticated travel hub has opened the wider region for exploration. Increasing numbers of travellers are discovering top-notch diving and trekking opportunities, fantastical landscapes and remarkable cultural diversity, but the smaller, outlying islands such as Sabu and Alor remain deliciously distant from the beaten track.

Traditional houses in Ratenggaro village, Sumba

Tea plantation, Nuwara Eliya

SRI LANKA

Modest in size compared to many of its Asian neighbours, Sri Lanka packs an astonishing array of attractions into its compact, pearl-shaped outline. The island lies just a few degrees from the equator and boasts an incredibly diverse range of landscapes, from the sultry tropical beaches, coconut plantations and lowland jungles of the coast to the cool green hill country, with its mist-shrouded mountains, crashing waterfalls and boundless tea plantations.

History runs deep in Sri Lanka, and a profusion of ancient monuments commemorates the island's role as one of the great bastions of the Buddhist faith. Massive stupas that rival the pyramids of Egypt in size dot the haunting ruined cities of Anuradhapura and Polonnaruwa, while living Buddhist traditions are evidenced in the vibrant city of Kandy.

Then there are the Sri Lankans themselves. Embroiled for a quarter of a century in one of the world's most pernicious civil wars and traumatized by the devastating 2004 Asian tsunami, and yet they remain among the world's most charming, welcoming and engaging people. Sri Lanka's citizens are happy to share their hard-won peace and growing prosperity with the visitors lucky enough to spend time on their enchanting island.

Traditional dancers in Kandy

Diyaluma Falls

Goyambokka Beach, Tangalle

Robed monks, Kelaniya Raja Maha Vihara Temple

TAJ MAHAL

Simply the world's greatest building, Shah Jahan's monument to love does not disappoint. Volumes have been written on its perfection, and its image adorns countless glossy brochures and guidebooks; nonetheless, the reality never fails to overwhelm all who see it, and few words can do it justice. A workforce of some twenty thousand men from all over Asia completed the Taj in 1653 after twenty years of toil, and it is undoubtedly the zenith of Mughal architecture.

Bengali poet Rabindranath Tagore described the Taj Mahal as "a teardrop on the face of eternity", and though its layout follows a distinctly Islamic theme, representing Paradise, it is above all a monument to romantic love. Shah Jahan built the Taj to enshrine the body of his favourite wife, Arjumand Bann Begum, better known by her official palace title, Mumtaz Mahal ("Chosen One of the Palace"). The emperor was devastated by her death, and set out to create an unsurpassed monument to her memory – the result is sublime.

Painting of Arjumand Bann Begum

Taj Mahal at sunset

Tomb of Shah Jahan and his wife, Mumtaz Mahal

Local and his camel outside the Taj Mahal

Huge stone face at Angkor Thom

View over Angkor Wat

Bas-relief depiction of King Suryavarman II at Angkor Wat

Monk at Ta Prohm

TEMPLES OF ANGKOR

The world-famous temples of Angkor dot the Cambodian countryside, rising out of the enveloping forest like the classic lost-in-the-jungle ancient ruins of every Hollywood filmmaker's wildest dreams. Top of most visitors' lists is the unforgettable Angkor Wat, with its five soaring towers hemmed in by a moat. The surreal Bayon, plastered with hundreds of superhuman faces, and the jungle temple of Ta Prohm, its crumbling ruins clamped in the grip of giant kapok trees, are also must-sees.

However many times you've seen it on film or in photographs, nothing readies you for the majesty of Angkor Wat. Dominated by five majestic, corncob towers, this masterpiece of Khmer architecture was built by Suryavarman II between around 1113 and 1150. Stunning from a distance, its intricacy becomes apparent as you approach, with every surface covered in fine detail. Throughout the day the colour of its stone changes with the light.

Fabrika – a multifunctional space set inside an old sewing factory

Rhike Park

Tbilisi National Gallery

Enjoying the sunshine

TBILISI

While the Georgian capital, Tbilisi, has long lured visionary types to its bohemian neighbourhoods, it's slipped under the tourist radar for years. That may have something to do with its turbulent recent history: although Georgia gained independence from the Soviet Union in 1991, there followed a period of civil war, violence and ethnic tensions.

Over the past decade, however, a new generation has reignited Tbilisi's cultural scene through a mix of local art galleries, exhibition spaces, music venues, concept stores and creative hubs. A growing crop of industrial-style hotels is springing up across the city, many set in Soviet-era factories and publishing houses. The food scene is thriving, too – innovative chefs have taken the helm in the kitchens of new restaurants, where they reimagine traditional Georgian cuisine with a modern twist. The revolution is underway.

Bridge of Peace

TOKYO

Tokyo is exactly what you think it is, and nothing like you expect. It is kimono-clad women stepping daintily along Asakusa streets, neon signs jostling for attention, white-gloved station attendants squeezing commuters into subway cars. It is narrow alleyways strung with a tangle of overhead cables, neighbourhood shrines with offerings of beer and satsumas, processions of school-children with identical backpacks. Ordered yet bewildering, Japan's pulsating capital will lead you a merry dance: this is Asia at its weirdest, straightest, prettiest, sleaziest and coolest, all at the same time.

With the eyes of the world turned to Tokyo for the Olympics, 2020 is an exciting year for Japan. This is the largest city ever to host the games, so visitors will have plenty to do and see between events, from sushi to sumo, geisha to gardens, neon to noodles. But what spectators are sure to remember most is the unforgettable kindness of Tokyoites, the Japanese philosophy of *omotenashi* – clunkily translated as "hospitality" – extended to everyone who comes here to celebrate.

Shinjuku Gyoen Garden

Sushi from Tsukiji Fish Market

Japanese sumo wrestlers

Shinjuku alleyway

Kimono-clad Tokyoite

Donkey cart, Merv

Wedding Palace, Ashgabat

One of Turkmenistan's famous golden horses

Darvaza gas crater

Yusuf Hamadani Mosque, Merv

TURKMENISTAN

Under leader Niyazov - famous for renaming the months after his own family, banning beards and gold teeth and outlawing opera - the secretive country of Turkmenistan retained communism long after the collapse of the Soviet system. Enormous gas reserves now boost its own economy rather than Moscow's, catapulting the capital Ashgabat to a shining beacon on the desert's edge - quite literally, as all public buildings must be clad in white marble, ideally Italian Carrara.

Linking China with Rome more than two thousand years ago was the Parthian Empire, whose early Silk Road capital Nisa lies just outside Ashgabat. Turkmen history is underpinned by the breeding of the famous Akhal-Teke horse - the country's national emblem, used for carrying people and news along the route. Known as "golden horses", these majestic animals have shimmering coats of brilliant shades to provide camouflage against a desert backdrop.

Elsewhere, UNESCO-endorsed Merv was once the Silk Road's largest city, its Buddhist temple, Christian church and Islamic mosque all showing different ways to heaven, while the fiery furnace in the desert at Darvaza - or the "Gateway to Hell" - is utterly spectacular.

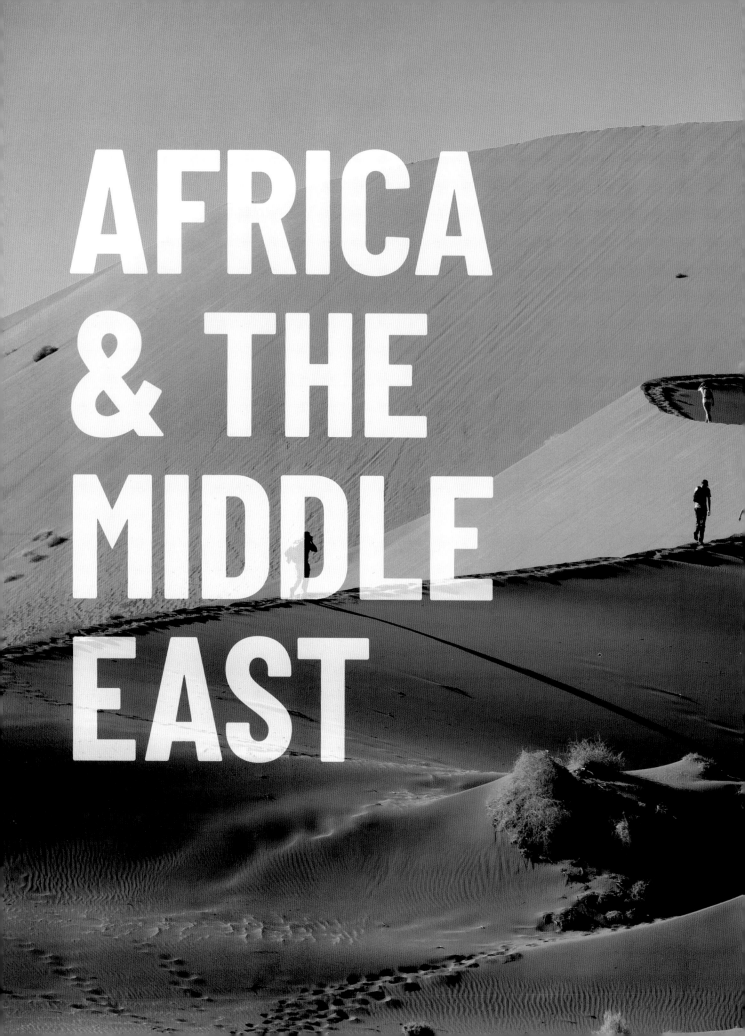

AFRICA & THE MIDDLE EAST

The ruined Egg cinema, which today hosts raves, art exhibitions and theatre productions

Gemmayzeh café

Bar on Gouraud Street

Martyrs' Square

BEIRUT

Beirut has an amazing early history that has seen the headland protect fleets of Phoenician biremes, Greek triremes, Roman galleys and Ottoman galleons. A hot spot for celebrities by the 1960s, in more recent years Beirut has become synonymous with the troubles in the Middle East, an image it's slowly shaking off with a blossoming cultural scene, an exciting East-meets-West outlook and sophisticated fashions, hip cafés and trendy galleries. On a calm day there is nowhere better to have a sumptuous restaurant meal with magnificent views, promenade along the bustling Corniche and party in the myriad nightclubs till the early hours.

Lebanon is a small country, and nowhere is more than 130km from the centrally placed capital – every sight can be visited on a day-trip. And in Lebanon, whatever the difficulties, life is lived to the max. As the locals say, "History, hedonism and hummus – what more do you need?"

Vineyards in the Constantia Valley

Long Street

Aerial view of Cape Town

Kiteboarding on Bloubergstrand

Bo-Kaap houses

CAPE TOWN

Cape Town is one of Africa's most beautiful, most romantic and most visited cities. Its physical setting is extraordinary, something its pre-colonial Khoikhoi inhabitants acknowledged when they referred to Table Mountain, the city's famous landmark, as Hoerikwaggo – the mountain in the sea. If the landscape doesn't take your breath away, its high-octane activities from paragliding to kitesurfing should do the trick, and that's before you've sampled the nightlife. Away from the thrills and pumping party scene, you'll find a city boasting fabulous beaches, rolling vineyards and fine museums.

Often referred to as the Mother City, Cape Town is truly cosmopolitan, evoking both Western and African sensibilities. The city centre's graceful Victorian, Georgian and Art Deco buildings will strike a chord of familiarity to European visitors, while North Americans may feel unexpectedly at home in Cape Town's expansive malls such as the V&A Waterfront. Equally, there are the vast and emphatically African townships that stretch east of the city centre, Islamic Cape Malay enclaves such as the richly atmospheric Bo-Kaap, and above all Long Street, the uncategorizable Afro-meets-Boho pulse of the city.

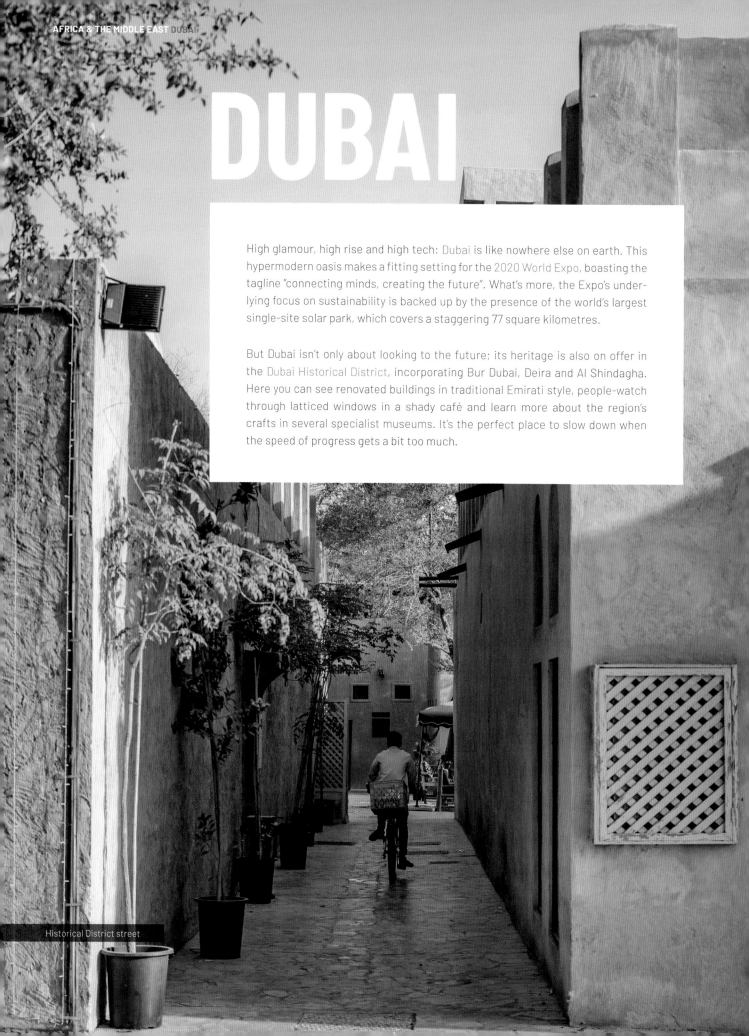

DUBAI

High glamour, high rise and high tech: Dubai is like nowhere else on earth. This hypermodern oasis makes a fitting setting for the 2020 World Expo, boasting the tagline "connecting minds, creating the future". What's more, the Expo's underlying focus on sustainability is backed up by the presence of the world's largest single-site solar park, which covers a staggering 77 square kilometres.

But Dubai isn't only about looking to the future; its heritage is also on offer in the Dubai Historical District, incorporating Bur Dubai, Deira and Al Shindagha. Here you can see renovated buildings in traditional Emirati style, people-watch through latticed windows in a shady café and learn more about the region's crafts in several specialist museums. It's the perfect place to slow down when the speed of progress gets a bit too much.

Historical District street

Dubai skyline

Museum of the Poet Al Oqaili

Inside the Old Fort

Celebrating Timkat festival

ETHIOPIA

An enigmatic and utterly beguiling country, Ethiopia has endless intrigue. From its unique, highly sociable cuisine – the basis of which is *injera*, a spongy sourdough pancake, piled high with piquant curries and stews and shared between friends – to its ancient language and curly Amharic script, there's very little that's familiar about this place, and it's all the better for it.

Ethiopia is a largely Orthodox Christian country, and its religious festivals and structures are something to behold. The sunken churches of Lalibela, hand-carved out of red rock below ground some nine hundred years ago, are an astonishing feat of engineering. Come January, the network of tunnels and staircases that connect all eleven fill up with thousands of worshippers dressed in white, celebrating the birth of Christ with a twelve-hour mass.

Elsewhere, you'll discover castles dating back to the sixteenth century, a curious coffee culture and an Ethio-jazz scene in the capital Addis Ababa like no other.

Traditional Ethiopian coffee ceremony

Illustrated Amharic bible

Rock-hewn Church of St George, Lalibela

Ethiopian spread

The Western Wall

Scuba divers in the Red Sea

Floating in the Dead Sea

Christian pilgrim on the Via Dolorosa

JERUSALEM

The Holy Land may be small in size, but it has had a disproportionate impact on world history over the last two thousand years. At its heart sits Jerusalem, one of the oldest and most famous cities on earth. Sacred to three great world religions – Judaism, Christianity and Islam – it is full of sights venerated by the faithful, notably the Western Wall, the mosque of the Dome of the Rock and the Via Dolorosa – the route taken by Christ on his way to the Crucifixion.

You don't have to be a believer to savour all this. And while Jerusalem itself is vibrant, absorbing and controversial – remaining at the centre of the Israeli-Palestinian conflict – it is also a well-placed base for visiting other legendary sites in the area, notably the Dead Sea, the Red Sea (with its crystal-clear waters excellent for scuba diving) and the Sinai Desert.

Dome of the Rock

MAASAI MARA NATIONAL RESERVE

Set at nearly 2000m above sea level, the Maasai Mara is a great wedge of undulating grassland in the remote, sparsely inhabited southwest of Kenya, right up against the Tanzanian border and an extension of the even bigger Serengeti National Park in Tanzania. This is a land of short grass and croton bushes, where the wind plays with the thick, green mantle after the rains and, nine months later, whips up dust devils from the baked surface. Maasai Mara's climate is relatively predictable, with ample rain, and the new grass supports an annual wildebeest migration of half a million animals from the dry plains of Tanzania.

At any time of year, the Mara has abundant wildlife. Whether you're watching the migration, a pride of lions hunting, a herd of elephants grazing in the marsh or hyenas squabbling with vultures over the carcass of a buffalo, you are conscious all the time of being in a realm apart. To travel through the reserve in August or September, when the wildebeest are in procession, feels like being caught up in the momentum of a historic event. There are few places on earth where animals hold such dazzling sway.

Cat nap: leopard in the Maasai Mara

Women in Antananarivo

Manual pollination of vanilla

Chameleon in Andasibe National Park

Ring-tailed lemur

MADAGASCAR

Madagascar is like nowhere else on earth. Set adrift in the middle of the Indian Ocean about 500km from Africa and almost ten times as distant from Asia, it is the world's fourth-largest island and the most isolated landmass of comparable proportions anywhere in the tropics. Culturally and ethnically, the Malagasy people have diverse origins, essentially being a fusion of Indonesian and African stock, but once liberally spiced with influences from Arabia, India, China, France and elsewhere.

For many visitors, the primary attraction of the island is its postcard-perfect beaches, turquoise lagoons, whispering palm plantations, craggy islets and snorkel-friendly coral reefs that adorn its 10,000km coastline. For adventurous travellers, however, Madagascar really comes into its own away from the beaches. This immense tropical island is sometimes referred to as the Eighth Continent on account of its unique biodiversity, which incorporates an estimated ten thousand animal and plant species found nowhere else in the world. Now protected in a network of roughly fifty official national parks and reserves, this diversity includes one hundred species of loveable lemur, and a similar tally of colourful chameleons and endemic birds.

Jemaa el Fna

Koutoubia Mosque and Minaret

Snake charmer

El Badi Palace

Saadian Tombs

MARRAKESH

Marrakesh – "Morocco City", as early foreign travellers called it – is the most exotic, mysterious and enchanting city this close to Europe. At its heart is the Jemaa el Fna, where a thrilling thousand-year-old nightly show unfolds like a magic carpet at sunset. There are acrobats and magicians, storytellers and snake charmers, as well as all manner of spontaneous entertainment in between. The city's architectural attractions are no less compelling: the magnificent ruins of the El Badi Palace, the delicate carving of the Saadian Tombs and, above all, the Koutoubia Minaret, the most perfect Islamic monument in North Africa.

At times daunting, occasionally maddening, always exhilarating, Marrakesh is all about getting lost, letting go and opening up to whatever experience or encounter comes your way.

MOUNT SINAI

The interior of the Sinai peninsula in Egypt is a stark, unforgiving place. Beneath a strikingly blue sky lie parched mountains, rocky outcrops and great expanses of barren sand, interspersed with isolated oases and crisscrossed by medieval pilgrimage routes. It is, in the truest sense, a landscape of biblical proportions.

In the south of this region, just a few hours' drive from the booming tourist resort of Sharm el-Sheikh, rises the magnificent 2285m Mount Sinai, venerated by Christians, Muslims and Jews alike as the site of God's unveiling of the Ten Commandments. Although there is some doubt about whether this red-and-grey granite peak is actually the site mentioned in the Bible, it is undeniably awe-inspiring – particularly the views from the summit, reached via 3750 knee-crunching "Steps of Repentance", or the easier but longer "camel path". Despite the crowds of pilgrims, travellers and Bedouin guides (and their camels), a night camped out here under a star-filled sky allows you to wake up to one of the most beautiful sunrises imaginable.

Mount Sinai at sunrise

Solitary oryx in the Namib Desert

Namib-Naukluft National Park

Giraffes in Etosha National Park

Sand dunes flanking the Atlantic coast

NAMIBIA

The oldest desert in the world makes for a mind-blowing adventure. Namibia is one of the driest places on earth, with an undulating blanket of sand dunes and red-tinged rock stretching all the way from the Atlantic coast inland and beyond its border with Botswana.

Walk among the jet-black, petrified forest that sits within the bright white mineral pan of Deadvlei – best viewed at sunrise when the towering dunes around it, the tallest in the world, turn striking reds and oranges as the light changes.

It's not all desert, though – there's a bounty of wildlife in Etosha National Park, where lions, elephants, giraffes and elegant oryx roam freely, often seen together at the many watering holes dotted throughout the plains. And at the end of the day, Namibia's sunsets steal the show. Every evening is a display of fiery yellows, reds and pinks – the world's best place for a sundowner.

Deadvlei

NGORONGORO CONSERVATION AREA

Despite the high tourist numbers, the hype and the expense, the Ngorongoro Conservation Area – designated a World Heritage Site in 1979 – lives up to all expectations. Ngorongoro's highlight is an enormous volcanic crater, formed by the same immense geological upheavals as the Great Rift Valley. Once a mountain as high as Kilimanjaro, about three million years ago Ngorongoro blew itself to bits, covering the Serengeti in ash while the crater floor sank into the mountain. Today, the rim stands at an impressive 2285m.

Ngorongoro provides one of the continent's most stunning backdrops for viewing a glut of wildlife, including the world's densest population of lions and spotted hyenas, several massive old tuskers and some of East Africa's last black rhinos.

Ngorongoro Crater

Spotted hyena

Lions grooming

Black rhinoceros

PETRA

Petra astounds. Tucked away in a remote valley basin in the heart of southern Jordan's Shara mountains and shielded from the outside world behind an impenetrable barrier of rock, this ancient city remains wreathed in mystery. Today, it's as if time has literally drawn a veil over Petra, which grew wealthy enough on the caravan trade to challenge the might of Rome: two millennia of wind and rain have blurred the sharp edges of its ornate Classical facades and rubbed away at its soft sandstone to expose vivid bands of colour beneath, putting the whole scene into soft focus.

The arrival never disappoints. The epic walk in, down the wadi and into the twisting narrow gorge known as the Siq, precedes an initial glimpse of the sun-lit Treasury which is as jaw-dropping as when Burckhardt "rediscovered" Petra over two hundred years ago. Smoothly eroded Nabataean tombs, with their swirling layers of multicoloured sandstone, imperiously dominate the later Roman Theatre. Walk along the Colonnaded Street then tackle the stepped climb to the remarkable rock-cut Monastery, carved from the mountain summit. Be prepared to have your imagination fired.

Approaching the Treasury

PYRAMIDS OF GIZA

Of the Seven Wonders of the ancient world, only three great Pyramids of Giza have withstood the ravages of time. No other monuments are so instantly recognized around the world, and for millions of people the Pyramids epitomize ancient Egypt. Yet comparatively few foreigners realize that there are at least 115 further pyramids spread across 70km of desert, from the outskirts of Cairo to the edge of the Fayoum Oasis. The mass of theories, claims and counterclaims about how and why the pyramids were built adds to the sense of mystery that surrounds them. During the daytime, the tourist hordes dispel the mystique, but visit at sunset, dawn or late at night and you'll find that their brooding majesty returns.

Camel in front of the Pyramids of Giza

SAHARA DESERT

The Sahara Desert conjures a string of romantic images: swirling sands, covered-up Bedouin, mirages, thirsty caravans stumbling upon an oasis set amid swaying palms. While little of this vision has any foundation in reality – the caravans have all but vanished and the Bedouin have traded their camels for Toyotas – not even the vestiges of modern humanity are capable of taming this majestic wilderness, where shifting sands can block roads for days and where the foolhardy can still meet death by the sting of a scorpion.

The Sahara spreads out across North Africa, covering an area of staggering proportions – 9,400,000 square kilometres and growing – hemmed in by the Atlas Mountains and the Mediterranean to the north, the Red Sea in the east, the Sahel in the south and the Atlantic in the west. The world's greatest expanse of desert is broken only by dots of green, where human habitation has survived the spread of sands, and temporary camps where Bedouin communities gather around their campfires. It is hard to overstate the scale and splendour of the desert, where the space, the sky and the silence are all colossal – and where the stark landscape and its hardy inhabitants continue to withstand the sands of time.

Camel trekking

Desert scorpion

Berber musician

Sunset in Stone Town

Street life

Locals taking a dip

House of Wonders

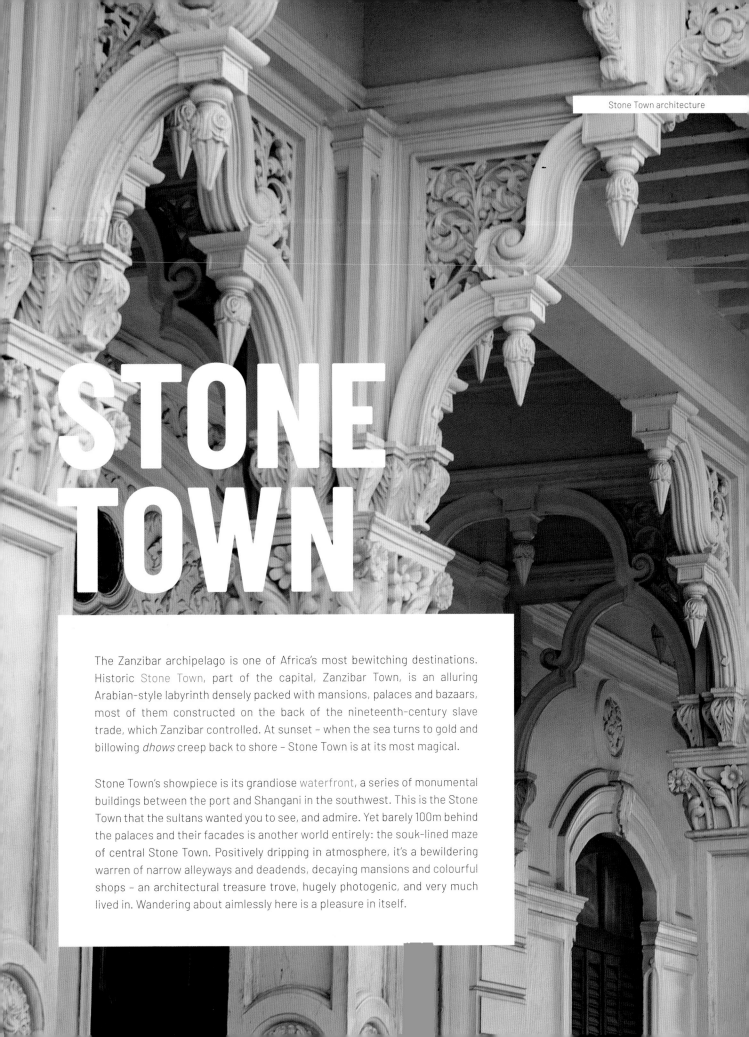

STONE TOWN

The Zanzibar archipelago is one of Africa's most bewitching destinations. Historic Stone Town, part of the capital, Zanzibar Town, is an alluring Arabian-style labyrinth densely packed with mansions, palaces and bazaars, most of them constructed on the back of the nineteenth-century slave trade, which Zanzibar controlled. At sunset – when the sea turns to gold and billowing *dhows* creep back to shore – Stone Town is at its most magical.

Stone Town's showpiece is its grandiose waterfront, a series of monumental buildings between the port and Shangani in the southwest. This is the Stone Town that the sultans wanted you to see, and admire. Yet barely 100m behind the palaces and their facades is another world entirely: the souk-lined maze of central Stone Town. Positively dripping in atmosphere, it's a bewildering warren of narrow alleyways and deadends, decaying mansions and colourful shops – an architectural treasure trove, hugely photogenic, and very much lived in. Wandering about aimlessly here is a pleasure in itself.

VICTORIA FALLS

Along with Mount Everest and the Grand Canyon, Victoria Falls – or Mosi-oa-Tunya ("the smoke that thunders") – ranks as one of the world's seven natural wonders. No matter how many pictures you've seen beforehand, nothing can prepare you for the awe-inspiring sight and deafening sound of the falls. The world's widest curtain of water crashes down a huge precipice, producing clouds of spray visible from afar, before squeezing into a zigzag of sheer-sided gorges as a torrent of turbulent rapids, carving its way to the Indian Ocean well over 1000km away.

Their dramatic setting on the Zambezi river – on the Zambia-Zimbabwe border – has also made Victoria Falls the undisputed adventure capital of Africa. There's an array of adrenaline-fuelled activities on offer, from whitewater rafting and bungee jumping to zip-lining and bodyboarding. Less touted are the stunning wildlife-viewing opportunities Victoria Falls affords: the national parks that line the serene banks of the Upper Zambezi are home to large mammals, such as elephant, lion, buffalo, giraffe and leopard, as well as a variety of antelope and more than 410 bird species.

Trees peering over Victoria Falls

ACROPOLIS

The rock of the Acropolis, crowned by the dramatic ruins of the Parthenon, is one of the archetypal images of Western culture. The first time you see it, rising above the traffic or from a distant hill, is extraordinary: foreign, and yet utterly familiar. As in other Greek cities, the Acropolis itself is simply the highest point of Athens, and this steep-sided, flat-topped crag of limestone, rising abruptly 100m from its surroundings, has made it the focus of the city during every phase of its development. Easily defensible and with plentiful water, its initial attractions are obvious – little wonder it served as home to one of the earliest known settlements in Greece in 5000 BC. Even now, with no function apart from tourism, the Acropolis is the undeniable heart of the city, around which everything else clusters, glimpsed at every turn.

Frieze on the Parthenon

Amphitheatre of the Acropolis

Acropolis at sunset

Erechtheum at the Acropolis

Palacios Nazaríes

The Alhambra seen from Mirador de San Nicolás

Exquisite tiling

The Alhambra bathed in light

Moorish arches

ALHAMBRA

While the rest of Europe was groping its way towards the Renaissance, a sophisticated Moorish civilization was flourishing in southern Spain. In its twilight splendour it created its most spectacular legacy, the Alhambra – an extraordinary palace-fortress overlooking the beautiful Andalucían city of Granada.

The Alhambra is one of the most sensual architectural creations in the world. Forbiddingly austere outside, it is all the opposite within – a stunning laby-

rinth of cool and shady halls, pavilions, chambers, elaborate gardens and trickling fountains – spaces that were intended as a whole to provide an earthly experience of paradise. The Alhambra's collection of geometric ornamentation in stucco and tilework is breathtaking.

A night visit shows the palace in another dimension as the play of shadows becomes part of the magic. The classic view of the Alhambra is from a square in the Albaicín – a *mirador* (lookout) in the city's labyrinthine Moorish quarter located on an adjacent hill.

Berlin nightlife

Gedenkstätte Berliner Mauer

Street art

The fall of the wall, November 9, 1989

BERLIN WALL

The scenes of August 13, 1961, when Berlin was cut in two, are still vivid in many people's minds. Literally overnight, not only were capitalism and communism divided, but families too. To Erich Honecker's East German regime, it was an "anti-Fascist protective wall"; to the rest of the world, it was a symbol of oppression.

The Berlin Wall, landmark of a divided city, finally fell on November 9, 1989, and East and West Berliners celebrated together for the first time in 28 years. The wall now belongs to history – although parts can still be seen. At the East Side Gallery in Friedrichshain, a 1.3km surviving stretch has been covered in political and satirical murals painted by artists from all over the world, while at the Gedenkstätte Berliner Mauer a 60m section of the Wall still stands in all its frightening might, together with a centre that keeps the story of the Wall alive using photos, sound recordings and information terminals.

In Berlin today there is hardly a trace of the old border crossings, yet nowhere else in Germany are the consequences of reunification felt so strongly. The city's 1989 rebirth is key to understanding Berlin's youthful vitality. The first wave of *post-Wende* ("turning-point") settlers – artists, squatters, musicians, DJs – set the edgy, alternative tone that still drives the city today.

CAPPADOCIA

Forged by wind and water, the otherworldly terrain of Cappadocia has become one of the star attractions of Turkey. Its hills are dotted with fantastical forms, honeycombed with cavern towns that give way to boulder-strewn plains. Ancient volcanic eruptions cloaked this Anatolian plateau in thick ash, which hardened into a soft rock that's since been contoured by the elements into cones, mushrooms, pillars and chimneys. In the fourth century AD, humans started to carve a labyrinth of cave dwellings and tunnels into, and beneath, the stone – some dug eighteen-storeys deep.

The subterranean towns of Derinkuyu and Kaymakli offer an insight into the vast underground complexes, while Göreme is dotted with cave churches adorned with seventh-century Byzantine frescoes. Pasabag valley is peppered with "fairy chimneys" – soaring cone-shaped formations that could be plucked straight from a fairy tale. One of the best experiences here is bedding down in a rockhewn hotel before taking a hot-air balloon ride to glimpse the jaw-dropping landscapes from above.

Uchisar Castle, Cappadocia

Stradun

Dubrovnik city walls

Old Town and port

Pile Gate

Dubrovnik's iconic red roofs

DUBROVNIK OLD TOWN

A walled, sea-battered city lying at the foot of a grizzled mountain, Dubrovnik is Croatia's most popular tourist destination, and it's not difficult to see why. An essentially medieval town reshaped by Baroque planners after the earthquake of 1667, Dubrovnik's historic core seems to have been suspended in time ever since. A labyrinth of tiny cobbled alleyways inside the Old Town gives way to bougainvillea-draped limestone buildings, housing a variety of restaurants and shops. One main thoroughfare runs through the melee: Stradun leads from Pile Gate, the main entrance to the city, to the Old Town Harbour, where ferries lead to lush islands just off shore.

The original city walls date back to the eighth century; modified and extended over the years, they now stand 25m high and stretch for some 2km. The walls are encrusted with towers and bastions, and it's impossible not to be struck by their remarkable size and state of preservation. Once you're on top, endless views extend over the mass of red-tiled roofs, the deep-blue Adriatic and the arid face of Srd Mountain.

The Quays

Kirwan's Lane

The Galway coast

Wild oysters

GALWAY

A 2020 European Capital of Culture, the delightful harbour city of Galway in western Ireland is a vibrant, fun-loving place known for its festivals, music and bars. Its town centre is compact and colourful, its cobbled streets lined with buskers who sing for their supper, atmospheric old buildings and traditional pubs ringing with live Irish music and good *craic*.

Medieval remnants such as the old city walls, the Spanish Arch and stone facades fronting artsy boutiques make a perfect backdrop for Galway's laidback, bohemian atmosphere. There's a passionate local food scene too, from cosy cafés, bistros and fine-dining restaurants to the delectable week-end market and September oyster festival. Make for Salthill to stroll along the seaside promenade fronting Galway Bay.

As the capital of the Gaelic West, this is the only city in the country where you might possibly hear Irish spoken on the streets. Galway also lies on the Wild Atlantic Way, making it the perfect jumping-off point for exploring the remote peninsulas of Connaught and Connemara, with their rugged shores, lochs and mountains.

GORGES DU VERDON

The breathtaking beauty and majesty of the Gorges du Verdon, also known as the Grand Canyon du Verdon, almost match its American counterpart, albeit on a much smaller scale. Peppered with spectacular viewpoints, plunging crevices up to 700m deep, and glorious azure-blue lakes, this area of Provence in France is absolutely irresistible. The river falls from Rougon at the top of the gorge, disappearing into tunnels, decelerating for shallow, languid moments and finally exiting in full, steady flow at the Pont du Galetas at the western end of the canyon. Alongside is the huge artificial Lac de Sainte-Croix, which is great for swimming when the water levels are high.

Moustiers-Ste-Marie is the loveliest village on the fringes of the gorge, occupying a magnificent site near its western end. Set high on a hillside, just out of sight of both canyon and lake, it straddles a plummeting stream that cascades between two golden cliffs. A star slung between them on a chain, originally suspended by a returning Crusader, just adds to its charms.

Boats traversing the Gorges du Verdon

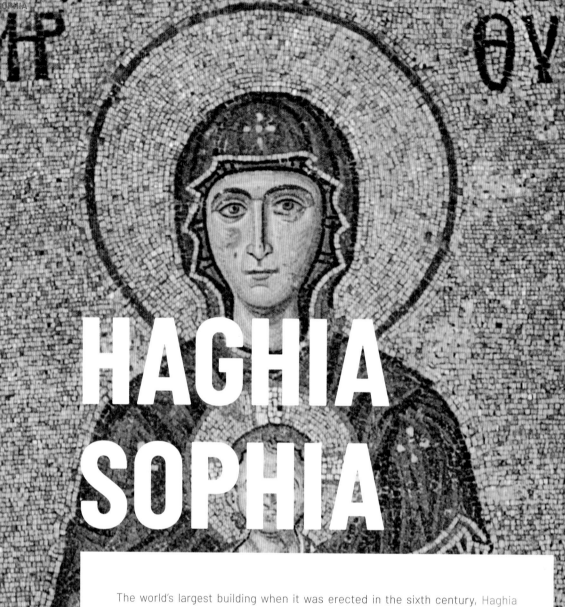

HAGHIA SOPHIA

The world's largest building when it was erected in the sixth century, Haghia Sophia – or the Church of the Holy Wisdom – has been a major influence on architecture ever since. Replete with elegant minarets – added during the centuries in which it served as an Ottoman mosque – it stands on a prominent high point of old Istanbul (the former Constantinople). Together with its equally beautiful neighbour, the Blue Mosque, Haghia Sophia has helped define this remarkable city that straddles Europe and Asia across the busy waterway of the Bosphorus. Inside, the Haghia Sophia dwarfs the visiting hordes, who stare in awe at its massive main dome 56m overhead. In the upstairs galleries, dazzling Byzantine mosaics hold sway.

Depiction of the Virgin Mary holding Jesus, Haghia Sophia

Boats on the Bosphorus

The Blue Mosque

Haghia Sophia

Vatnajökull ice cave

Siglufjörður

Trendy restaurant, Reykjavik

View to Ísafjörður in the West Fjords

The Blue Lagoon

ICELAND

With lunar lava fields, creaking glaciers and electric-blue geothermal pools, Iceland is famed for its breathtaking landscapes. It's a place of dramatic contrasts: bleak and blasted, yet intensely beautiful, full of grinding ice and fiery eruptions, with a tiny capital city that generates a huge amount of quirky, energetic culture. Most visitors fly into Reykjavík, exploring its cutting-edge art galleries, cool cafés and New Nordic food haunts, before venturing out to the mist-shrouded Blue Lagoon and Golden Circle.

Fewer people travel north, but venturing off the beaten track pays off: this wild, untamed area of the island is contoured by jagged mountains, dazzling fjords and ice-swept valleys. Hire a 4WD and take a road trip to the desolate hinterlands of the West Fjords, scoping out turquoise lakes and thunderous waterfalls along the way. You're more likely to bump into shaggy Icelandic horses than people on the remote Tröllaskagi peninsula, while these northern waters are filled with minke and humpback whales. And, of course, part of the lure is chasing the elusive Aurora Borealis as it casts green streaks across the inky sky.

KAMNIŠKE-SAVINJA ALPS

Northern Slovenia's Kamniške-Savinja Alps are among the most stunning and least spoilt mountain ranges in Europe, a magical landscape embracing imperious limestone peaks, sweeping pastoral valleys and crystalline rivers and waterfalls. Hiking, mountain-climbing and cycling are all popular here, while in winter the snowy peaks are crisscrossed by ski runs.

The region's siren draw is the impossibly picturesque Logarska dolina (Logar Valley). Formed during the Ice Age, the 7km-long U-shaped glaciated valley features a level, green valley floor covered with flower-speckled meadows and beech woods, enclosed by step-like cliff sides riddled with glacial boulders, waterfalls, springs, streams and a majestic wreath of jagged grey peaks, most of which top 2000m. Velika Planina, a broad alpine plateau of grassy slopes, sinkholes and dwarf pines – as well as being one of Slovenia's prime dairy farming regions – is another highlight; villages hereabouts are distinguished by dozens of silvery-grey herdsmen's huts, unique for their conical, shingled roofs which extend like witches' hats almost all the way down to ground level. Nearby, the clear blue Kamniške Bistrica river cuts its way through a series of lovely gorges.

Kamniške Bistrica river spring

Logarska dolina view

Huts on the Velika Planina

Enjoying the Logarska dolina

Traditional Sami woman

Ice hotel room

Winter sunset

Camping in the Arctic wilderness

LAPLAND

Deep in the Finnish Arctic, Lapland is one of the most magical parts of the world, filled with juxtaposition and wonder: gorgeous coniferous forests fronting barren tundral wastelands, fast-flowing rivers and rapids alongside tranquil campsites, man-made glass-roof igloo hotels for viewing the outstanding Northern Lights, and Sami nomads proudly melding their traditional lives with smartphones and snowmobiles. It is without a doubt the one place in Finland that most captures the imagination and inspires the senses.

As you progress northwards the trees become spindlier, the forests more sparse, the settlements fewer, the hills more numerous – until you reach the bare-topped fells of northern Lapland. Up above the ever-descending tree line, vegetation begins to creep and crawl – dwarf juniper and willow and miniature birch clinging to the fellsides among the mosses and the lichens, the minuscule campions and tiny saxifrages.

The Northern Lights over a frozen forest

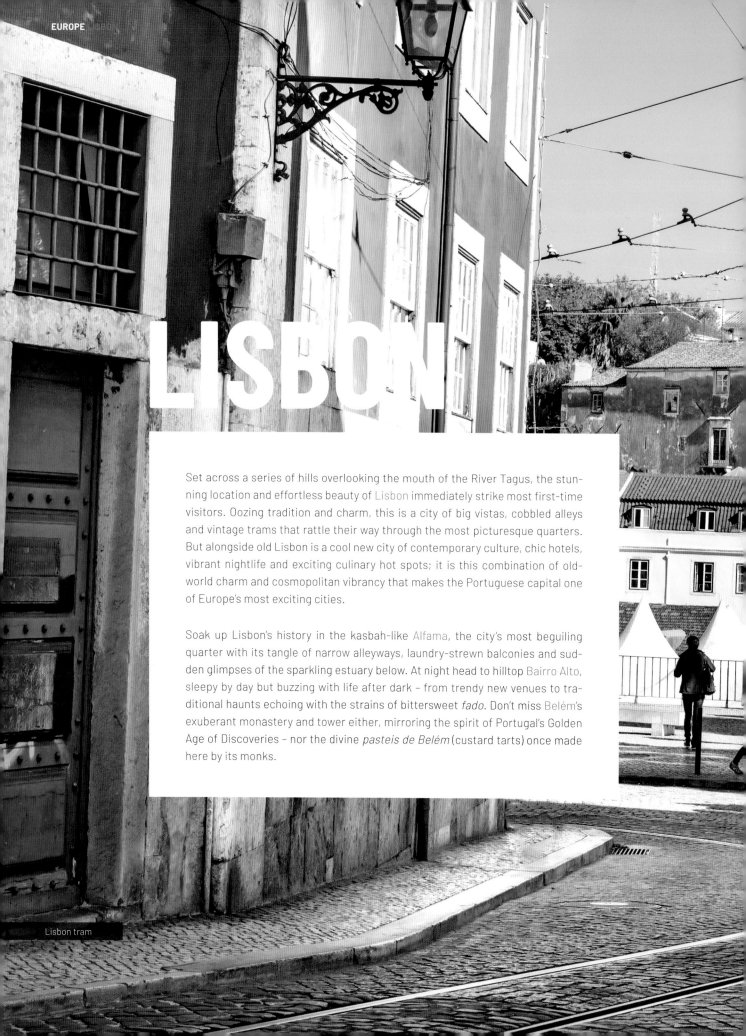

LISBON

Set across a series of hills overlooking the mouth of the River Tagus, the stunning location and effortless beauty of Lisbon immediately strike most first-time visitors. Oozing tradition and charm, this is a city of big vistas, cobbled alleys and vintage trams that rattle their way through the most picturesque quarters. But alongside old Lisbon is a cool new city of contemporary culture, chic hotels, vibrant nightlife and exciting culinary hot spots; it is this combination of old-world charm and cosmopolitan vibrancy that makes the Portuguese capital one of Europe's most exciting cities.

Soak up Lisbon's history in the kasbah-like Alfama, the city's most beguiling quarter with its tangle of narrow alleyways, laundry-strewn balconies and sudden glimpses of the sparkling estuary below. At night head to hilltop Bairro Alto, sleepy by day but buzzing with life after dark – from trendy new venues to traditional haunts echoing with the strains of bittersweet *fado*. Don't miss Belém's exuberant monastery and tower either, mirroring the spirit of Portugal's Golden Age of Discoveries – nor the divine *pasteis de Belém* (custard tarts) once made here by its monks.

Lisbon tram

CARREIRA N

565

Primrose Hill facades

LONDON

London is a thrilling place. Monuments from the city's glorious past are everywhere, from medieval banqueting halls and the great churches of Christopher Wren to eclectic Victorian architecture. You can relax in quiet Georgian squares, explore the narrow alleyways of the City of London, wander along the riverside walkways, and uncover the quirks of what is still identifiably a collection of villages. Stretching for more than 50km from east to west, London is incredibly diverse, ethnically and linguistically, offering cultural and culinary delights from right across the globe.

The UK capital's traditional sights – Big Ben, Westminster Abbey, Buckingham Palace, St Paul's Cathedral, the Tower of London and so on – continue to draw in millions of tourists every year. Things change fast though, and the regular emergence of new attractions ensures there's plenty to do. With Tate Modern and the Shard, the city boasts the world's most popular modern art museum and Western Europe's tallest building. And the city continues to grow, its cultural, nightlife and culinary scenes pushing ever onwards into neighbourhoods once well beyond the tourist radar.

Tower of London

Tate Modern

London bar

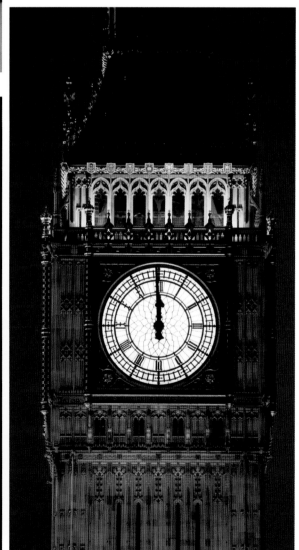

Big Ben

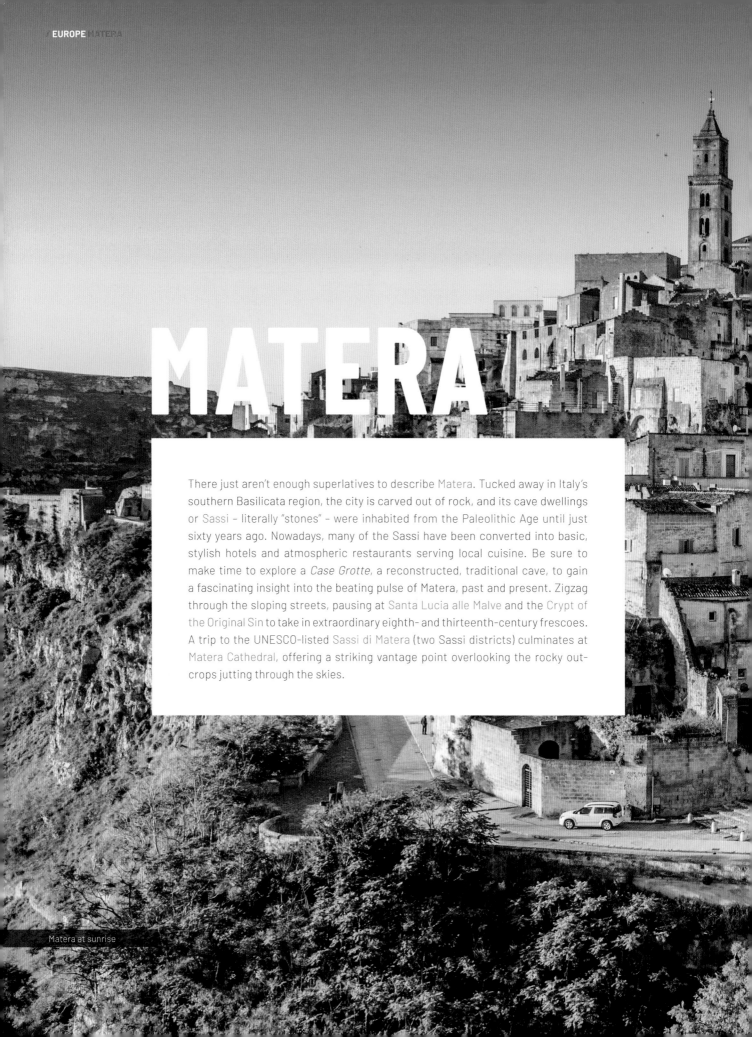

MATERA

There just aren't enough superlatives to describe Matera. Tucked away in Italy's southern Basilicata region, the city is carved out of rock, and its cave dwellings or Sassi – literally "stones" – were inhabited from the Paleolithic Age until just sixty years ago. Nowadays, many of the Sassi have been converted into basic, stylish hotels and atmospheric restaurants serving local cuisine. Be sure to make time to explore a *Case Grotte*, a reconstructed, traditional cave, to gain a fascinating insight into the beating pulse of Matera, past and present. Zigzag through the sloping streets, pausing at Santa Lucia alle Malve and the Crypt of the Original Sin to take in extraordinary eighth- and thirteenth-century frescoes. A trip to the UNESCO-listed Sassi di Matera (two Sassi districts) culminates at Matera Cathedral, offering a striking vantage point overlooking the rocky out-crops jutting through the skies.

Matera at sunrise

Geirangerfjord

NORWEGIAN FJORDS

The deep gorges of the fjord landscape, with crystal-clear bright-blue waters, cascading waterfalls and endless open vistas, is enough to take the breath away of even the most jaded world traveller. Views such as that from Preikestolen (Pulpit Rock), with a sheer drop of over 600m down to the Lysefjord below, or the Lofoten Wall, as the dark, forbidding cliff wall of the Lofoten Islands is known, are sights that have converted many a visitor into a firm Norway enthusiast. The tiny hamlet of Geiranger, with only three hundred inhabitants, receives around 700,000 visitors a year, who come to enjoy the magic and splendour of narrow Geirangerfjord, without the place seeming too crowded. There is always a sense of space and room to roam in Norway.

Norway's long coastline is punctuated by more than one thousand fjords, which reach all the way from Oslo in the southeast to the Arctic north. The most dramatic are those found along the west coast, with steep mountain walls rising up from the water, and small farms clinging to every ledge and hectare of green. The fjords are beautiful, timeless and everyone's idea of the soul of Norway.

Preikestolen

Nordland fishing boat

Colourful village near Bergen

Lofoten Islands

Musée d'Orsay

Paris bistro

The Louvre

Panorama from Notre-Dame

Pompidou Centre

PARIS

Capital of romance, food, intellectuals and philosophers, famed for its historic buildings and monuments and for that indefinable *je ne sais quoi* that makes up French chic, Paris is a city that likes to live up to its myths. The very fabric of the place is exquisite, with its magnificent avenues and atmospheric little backstreets, its grand formal gardens and intimate neighbourhood squares.

The city is divided into twenty arrondissements in a spiral, centred on the Louvre. Through the heart of the city flows the Seine, skirting the pair of islands where Paris was founded. The historic pillars of the city, Notre-Dame cathedral and the royal palace of the Louvre, stand on the riverbank, along with one of the world's most distinctive landmarks – the Eiffel Tower. The Louvre is one of the world's truly outstanding museums, while the art collections of the Musée d'Orsay and Pompidou Centre are unrivalled.

Portheras Cove

Mousehole village

Filming *Poldark* in Charlestown

Surf's up

PENWITH

Penwith – the craggy, westernmost tip of Cornwall in the UK – crams huge variety into its petite dimensions. The wind-flayed northern coast displays a clear kinship with the rugged Atlantic seaboard of Ireland, while just 10km away the balmy southern shoreline has more in common with the Mediterranean. International TV audiences have been getting a taste of the Penwith landscape in recent years, thanks to its role as the backdrop for *Poldark*. But sheer isolation protects it from the over-commercialization of other, more accessible stretches of the Cornish coast. The main town, Penzance, is an authentic, offbeat base, with a lively arts scene and a burgeoning reputation among foodies, while the coastal footpath offers superb walking, passing ruined mine buildings and perfect beaches, some still undiscovered by Instagrammers. But the real untapped travel secret is inland Penwith, with its ridge of granite moorland, scattered farming hamlets and astonishing wealth of prehistoric monuments.

Mên-an-Tol

PRAGUE

Few other European capitals look quite as beautiful as Prague, with some six hundred years of architecture virtually untouched by natural disaster or war. Straddling the winding River Vltava, with a steep wooded hill to one side, the city retains much of its medieval layout, and its rich mantle of Baroque, Rococo and Art Nouveau buildings have successfully escaped the vanities and excesses of modern development.

Prague is divided into two unequal halves by the river, which meanders through the heart of the Czech capital and features one of its most enduring landmarks, Charles Bridge. Built during the city's medieval golden age, this stone bridge, with its parade of Baroque statuary, still forms the chief link between the more central old town, or Staré Město, on the right bank, and Prague's hilltop castle on the left.

The castle is a vast complex, which towers over the rest of the city and supplies the classic picture-postcard image of Prague. Spread across the slopes below are the wonderful cobbled streets and secret walled gardens of Malá Strana, little changed in the two hundred years since Mozart walked them.

Charles Bridge

Church of Our Lady before Týn

Wolfgang Amadeus Mozart waxwork at the Grévin Prague

Prague's bridges

State Historical Museum

Guard at the Tomb of the Unknown Soldier

Lenin's Mausoleum

The State Historical Museum, Kremlin and Red Square

RED SQUARE

Moscow's Red Square is Russia's epicentre, a witness to medieval executions, May 1st parades of ballistic missile launchers and a million Russian wedding photographs. Steeped in history, it is home to the State Historical Museum, Lenin's Mausoleum and the magnificent St Basil's Cathedral, while close by are relics of the tsarist era – the Old English Court, Old Merchant's Quarters and the Stock Exchange.

The Old Russian word *krasny* translates as both "beautiful" and "red", and Russia's main public space was meant to be called "Beautiful Square". Whatever its name, Red Square has long been the heart of ceremonial Russia: a place of celebration and public execution, a stage for leaders' appearances and the main hub for trade, news and gossip. The vast expanse (700m long and 130m wide) is enclosed by the Kremlin walls, the birthday-cake facades of GUM (State Department Store) and the State Historical Museum, with the riotous colours and forms of the Church of the Intercession on the Moat (St Basil's) rising on the fourth side.

St Basil's Cathedral

The Pantheon at night

Temple of Saturn, Roman Forum

Spiral staircase in the Vatican Museums

Trevi Fountain

ROME

Dubbed the Eternal City by poets and artists, Rome inspires the mind, appeals to the senses and captures the heart. Its eras crowd in on top of one another to a remarkable degree: there are medieval churches atop ancient basilicas and palaces, houses and apartment blocks that incorporate fragments of Roman columns and inscriptions, and roads and piazzas that follow the lines of ancient amphitheatres and stadiums.

Rome is an immense outdoor museum, and it's not an easy place to absorb on one visit. The city packs in a staggering number of iconic sights: the Colosseum, the most recognizable and perhaps the greatest ancient Roman monument of them all; the Roman Forum, the majestic ruins of the civic centre of Ancient Rome; Trevi Fountain; Piazza di Spagna, with the Spanish Steps and Keats-Shelley House; the Pantheon, Rome's most intact ancient sight; and the Vatican Museums – meriting a lifetime's study in their own right but most famed for Michelangelo's breathtaking ceiling in the Sistine Chapel.

Part of Rome's allure is stumbling across things by accident and gradually piecing the city together – just remember to pause at the superb pizzerias and *gelaterie* along the way.

Sagrada Família facade

Exterior statues

Intricate relief carving

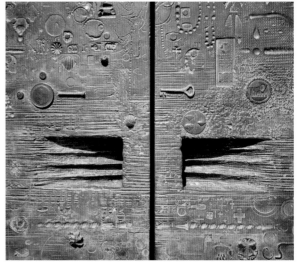

Religious door inscription

SAGRADA FAMÍLIA

Antoni Gaudí's unfinished masterpiece is one of Spain's truly essential sights. As work on the Basílica de la Sagrada Família races towards completion, and its extraordinary towers climb ever closer towards the heavens, the glorious, overpowering church of the "Sacred Family" is now more than ever a symbol for Barcelona, and even the coldest hearts will find it inspirational in both form and spirit.

Though work began in 1882 by public subscription, Antoni Gaudí took over on the Sagrada Família two years later. When he died – after being hit by a tram – in 1926, all Barcelona turned out for his funeral procession, after which Gaudí was buried in the Sagrada Família crypt. Only one facade of the church was then complete. Work stalled during the Civil War, with most of Gaudí's original plans and models lost in the turmoil. Construction finally restarted, amid great controversy, in the 1950s.

Even if the builders fail to meet their current target of finishing the church to mark the centenary of Gaudí's death in 2026, it looks like the Sagrada Família will finally be completed within the next decade.

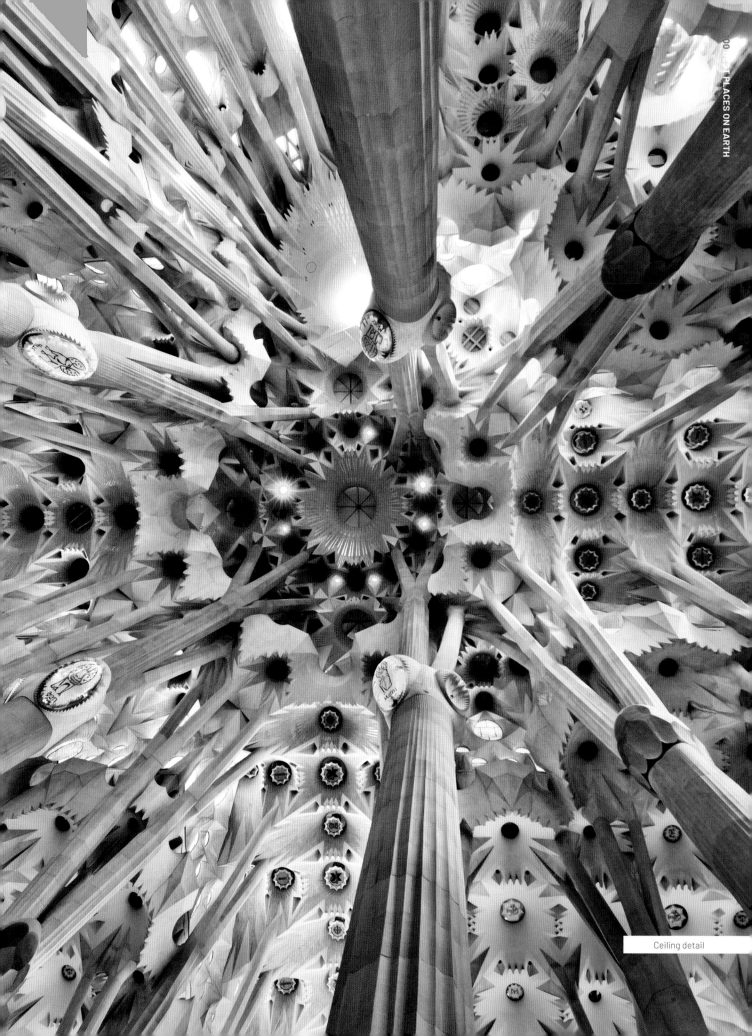

Ceiling detail

SAXON SWITZERLAND

Honey-coloured sandstone cliffs and over a thousand rock pinnacles tower above the pine trees and the snaking Elbe River in Saxon Switzerland (Sächsische Schweiz) in Germany. This wild area, set amid forested hills right on the Czech border and much of it protected as a national park, inspired many of Germany's Romantic-era painters and composers. More recently, it provided some of the dramatic landscapes and Mitteleuropean architectural features in Wes Anderson's *Grand Budapest Hotel.*

Historic paddle steamers and trains from Dresden stop off at several quaint riverside villages and the main town of Bad Schandau, with the park information office – trains between Berlin and Prague stop here too – making it an easy day-trip destination. Despite attracting shiploads of visitors on sunny days, the park is large enough to absorb the summer crowds who come to hike, bike, canoe or simply to wallow in a spa and eat cake.

Short hikes lead steeply up to famed sights – the bridge across the Bastei rock formation and the majestic Königstein fortress – both offering great panoramas over the Elbe valley. More challenging trails pass through caves, up stairs in moss-covered ravines and across steep rock faces to plateaus with magnificent views.

Bastei Bridge

SCOTTISH HIGHLANDS AND ISLANDS

The bleak yet beautiful Scottish Highlands feel like nowhere else in Britain. Here the weather is as changing as the scenery: a combination of dramatic mountains, remote glens, dark lochs and tumbling rivers surrounded on three sides by a magnificent coastline. Although the landscape is the main attraction, so too is the enduring sense of remoteness; the vast peat bogs in the north are among the most extensive and unspoilt wilderness areas in Europe and some of the west-coast crofting villages can still be reached only by boat.

The splendour of the Highlands would be bare without the islands off the west and north coasts. Assorted in size, flavour and accessibility, the long chain of rocky Hebrides which necklace Scotland's Atlantic shoreline includes Mull and its nearby pilgrimage centre of Iona; Islay and Jura, famous for their wildlife and whisky; Skye, where the snow-tipped peaks of the Cuillin rise above deep sea lochs; and the Western Isles, an elongated archipelago that is the country's last bastion of Gaelic language and culture. Off the north coast, Orkney and Shetland, both with a rich Norse heritage, offer some of the country's wildest scenery, finest birdwatching and best archeological sites.

Sligachan river, Skye

Shetland puffin

Iona Abbey

Scotch whisky

Peterhof

Bank Bridge lions

The Church of the Saviour on the Spilled Blood

The Winter Palace

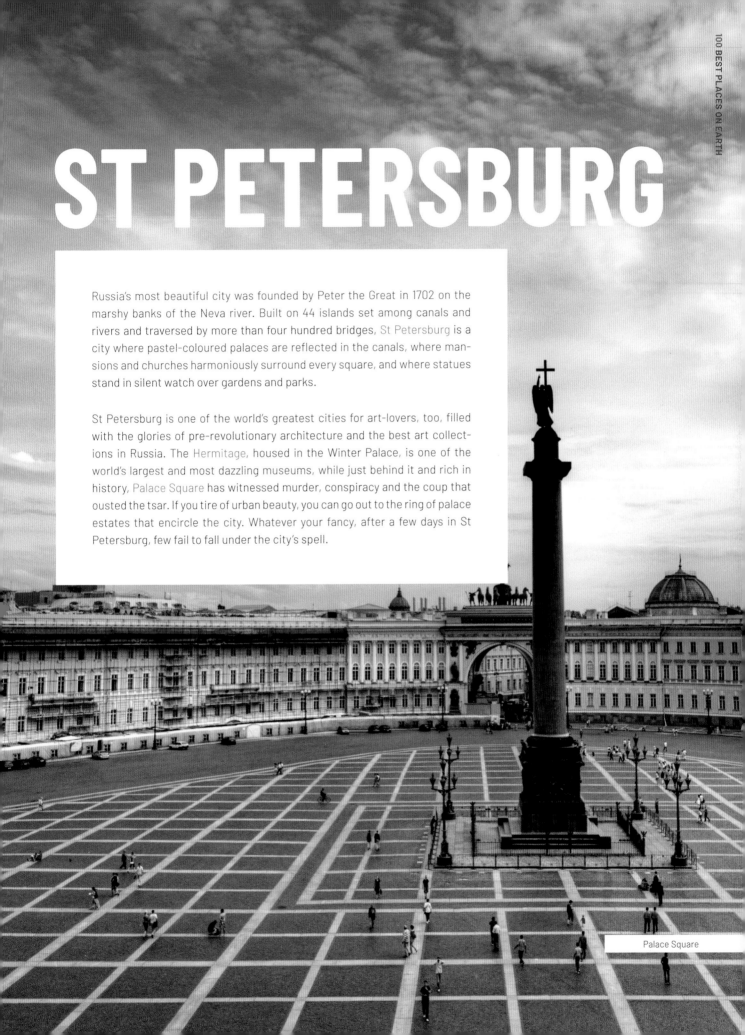

ST PETERSBURG

Russia's most beautiful city was founded by Peter the Great in 1702 on the marshy banks of the Neva river. Built on 44 islands set among canals and rivers and traversed by more than four hundred bridges, St Petersburg is a city where pastel-coloured palaces are reflected in the canals, where mansions and churches harmoniously surround every square, and where statues stand in silent watch over gardens and parks.

St Petersburg is one of the world's greatest cities for art-lovers, too, filled with the glories of pre-revolutionary architecture and the best art collections in Russia. The Hermitage, housed in the Winter Palace, is one of the world's largest and most dazzling museums, while just behind it and rich in history, Palace Square has witnessed murder, conspiracy and the coup that ousted the tsar. If you tire of urban beauty, you can go out to the ring of palace estates that encircle the city. Whatever your fancy, after a few days in St Petersburg, few fail to fall under the city's spell.

Palace Square

Gamla Stan

Relaxing outside Stockholm Public Library

Stockholm street

Museum of Modern Art (Moderna Museet)

Houseboats in the sunshine

STOCKHOLM

Without a shadow of a doubt, Stockholm is one of the most beautiful cities in Europe. It's built on no fewer than fourteen islands, where the fresh water of Lake Mälaren meets the brackish Baltic Sea, so clean air and open space are in plentiful supply here. One-third of the area within the city limits is made up of water, while another comprises parks and woodlands. As a result, the Swedish capital is one of Europe's saner cities and a delightful place in which to spend time. Broad boulevards lined with elegant buildings are reflected in the deep blue water, and rows of painted wooden houseboats bob gently alongside the cobbled waterfront. Natural beauty, though, is just one of the city's charms. Stockholm also has a glittering array of monuments, museums and restaurants, as well as a buzzing commercial heart and a cutting-edge start-up scene.

UTRECHT

With a bustling medieval centre characterized by sunken canals, a 112m-high gothic cathedral tower, narrow pedestrianized streets packed with shops and a flourishing restaurant and nightlife scene, Utrecht is a delightful university town. Just 25 minutes by train from the capital, Amsterdam, it feels a world away – with students on rusty bikes dominating the streets, it's easy to get a real feel of Dutch city life.

West of the Dom cathedral, the lively Oudegracht canal is lined with two levels of restaurants, terraces and shops, and features two castle-like medieval houses. Just to the east, stroll along the calm residential Nieuwegracht towards the Centraal Museum, which features the world's largest collection of Rietveld designs. Tours of the UNESCO-listed Rietveld Schröder House in the suburbs show just how revolutionary 1920s Rietveld architecture was. The newly renovated train station area and the state-of-the-art TivoliVredenburg music complex represent the new Utrecht; canals that were filled in to make way for roads here fifty years ago are now attractive waterways once again.

The countryside around Utrecht is easily explored along well-marked bicycle routes; pedal past impressive fortresses or along the new 20km De Stijl route to Amersfoort, passing ten sculptures inspired by artists Rietveld and Mondriaan.

Oudegracht canal

Basilica di San Marco

VENICE

The first-time visitor to Venice arrives full of expectations, most of which turn out to be well founded. All the photographs you've seen of the Palazzo Ducale, of the Basilica di San Marco, of the palaces along the Canal Grande – they've simply been recording the truth. Its lagoon setting, its blend of East and West, its role as a great maritime republic and its rich tapestry of art and architecture make Venice visually and culturally unique. It survives today against all odds: the only city in the world built entirely on water.

Start in Piazza San Marco, the world's most eulogized square, then take a slow boat down the Canal Grande to admire the rich parade of palaces. Spare time for the quieter side of Venice too, away from the crowds, and lose yourself in a maze of hidden passageways, quiet canals and sunlit squares.

After dark, this floating city is bewitchingly romantic. As the sun sinks, candles are lit, bars awaken, music drifts from churches and the rosy marble facade of the Doge's Palace glows in the evening light. Those with deep pockets should splash out on a gondola and glide silently through the moonlight.

Canal Grande

Piazza San Marco

Venice canal

Doge's Palace

Hall of Mirrors

Gardens of Versailles

Inside the Grand Trianon château

Ceiling painting in Salon d'Hercule

Latona Fountain

VERSAILLES

The Sun King of France did nothing by halves. Driven by envy of his finance minister's château at Vaux-le-Vicomte, the young Louis XIV recruited the same design team - architect Le Vau, painter Le Brun and gardener Le Nôtre - to create a palace a hundred times bigger. The result, Versailles, is the palace against which all other palaces are judged. The building, with its endless gilded chambers, speaks of unlimited royal power, while its landscaped grounds epitomize the Enlightenment attitude that human beings have been put on earth to subdue nature.

In its heyday, Versailles was the headquarters of every arm of state, a community of twenty thousand people from statesmen and sycophants to stable boys. It is now one of the biggest attractions in France, visited by more than seven million people annually. But it's at its very best on Saturday nights in summer, when the monumental fountains are floodlit and set to Baroque music.

USA,
MEXICO &
CANADA

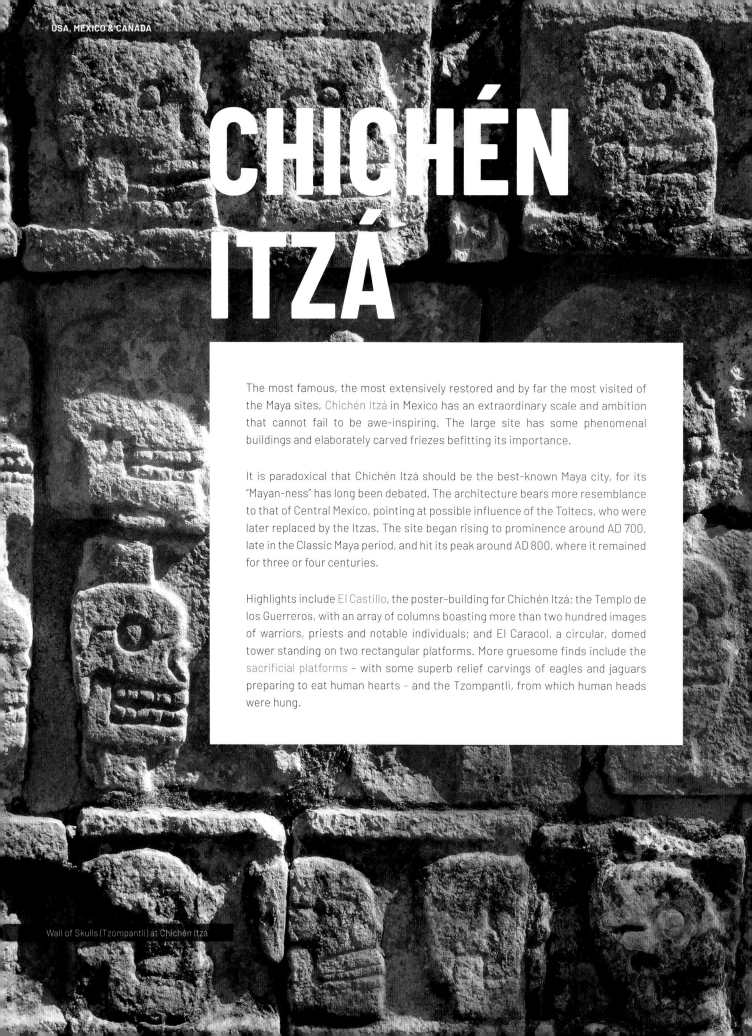

CHICHÉN ITZÁ

The most famous, the most extensively restored and by far the most visited of the Maya sites, Chichén Itzá in Mexico has an extraordinary scale and ambition that cannot fail to be awe-inspiring. The large site has some phenomenal buildings and elaborately carved friezes befitting its importance.

It is paradoxical that Chichén Itzá should be the best-known Maya city, for its "Mayan-ness" has long been debated. The architecture bears more resemblance to that of Central Mexico, pointing at possible influence of the Toltecs, who were later replaced by the Itzas. The site began rising to prominence around AD 700, late in the Classic Maya period, and hit its peak around AD 800, where it remained for three or four centuries.

Highlights include El Castillo, the poster-building for Chichén Itzá; the Templo de los Guerreros, with an array of columns boasting more than two hundred images of warriors, priests and notable individuals; and El Caracol, a circular, domed tower standing on two rectangular platforms. More gruesome finds include the sacrificial platforms – with some superb relief carvings of eagles and jaguars preparing to eat human hearts – and the Tzompantli, from which human heads were hung.

Wall of Skulls (Tzompantli) at Chichén Itzá

El Castillo

El Caracol

Templo de los Guerreros

Maroon Lake

Mural at Denver Central Market

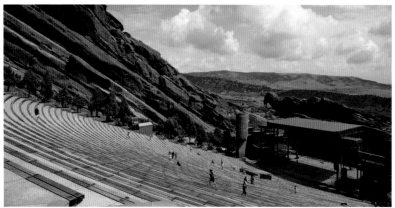

Red Rocks amphitheatre

Trail Ridge Road sunset

DENVER AND COLORADO

It's impossible not to have a good time in Colorado. Whether you're biking between brewpubs on Breckenridge's craft beer trail, hiking in the wilderness, exploring ancient Native American cliff dwellings or driving across the Continental Divide along the Trail Ridge Road – the highest paved road on the continent – you're surrounded by gorgeous Rocky Mountain scenery.

For more urban pleasures, the nightlife in Denver is second to none, with dozens of great bars and restaurants oozing laidback, Colorado cool. Its lively arts scene, from the architecturally stunning Denver Art Museum to the vivid street murals of the RiNo district, takes a leap into the cutting edge in 2020 with the opening of Meow Wolf, a mind-blowing immersive art installation. Leave the city buzz behind and head to Red Rocks, the world's finest open-air amphitheatre, for a concert under the stars or a morning yoga session, then venture on into Colorado's glorious mountains.

Denver Art Museum

GRAND CANYON

Although almost five million people visit Grand Canyon National Park every year, the canyon itself remains beyond the grasp of human imagination. No photograph, no statistics, can prepare you for such immensity. Billions of years of the earth's geologic history is frozen in bright bands of pink, beige, orange, rust and gold on the canyon walls. Peer into the abyss to glimpse a sliver of the Colorado River, nearly 2km below, which carved out the canyon some six billion years ago. By contrast, the national park – a UNESCO World Heritage Site – turned a mere one hundred in 2019.

Spend at least a full day here, watching the colours change in the shifting light. The vast majority of visitors come to the South Rim and linger at the viewpoints, spotting rare California condors soaring on the breeze, though the North Rim can be a lot more evocative by virtue of its isolation. Wherever you go, you are gazing at one of the Seven Wonders of the Natural World. Breathe it in.

A Grand Canyon sunrise

Wood End Light, Cape Cod

MASSACHUSETTS

Massachusetts has a special talent for looking backwards and forwards at the same time. The coastal town of Plymouth was home to some of America's earliest English settlers, and 2020 marks four hundred years since the arrival of the Pilgrims, as they came to be known, and the founding of the Plymouth Colony. The anniversary will be observed with a series of cultural events and festivals throughout the year.

But the state has a penchant for the novel too. Cambridge, home to lauded Harvard University and MIT, imbibes the creative spirit of its students. Boston, meanwhile, boasts avant-garde art galleries and the world's first robotic restaurant alongside its famed Freedom Trail, which chronicles the American Revolution.

Throw in Cape Cod's champagne coastline, the Berkshires' rural charm and a smattering of quaint small towns, and this New England state will have you hooked.

Museum of Fine Arts, Boston

Mayflower II replica, Plymouth

Harvard University graduates

Quincy Market restaurant, Boston

Rum Boogie Cafe, Memphis

Southern cuisine

Elvis's house, Graceland

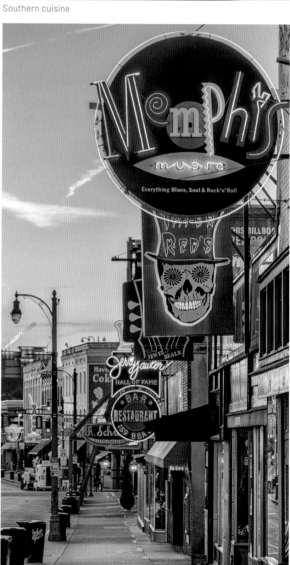

Neon lights on Beale Street

MEMPHIS AND THE DEEP SOUTH

Memphis is one of the best-sounding cities on earth – and it wears its musical heart on its sleeve. There's Graceland, the delightfully flamboyant former home of Elvis Presley, as well as pulsing Beale Street, with its snug blues clubs and raucous piano bars. The newly launched Tennessee Music Pathways spools into the wider state, joining up these musical bastions with other spots relating to soul, bluegrass, jazz and country.

But this city, and indeed the whole of the Deep South, is more than its music. The food is worth travelling for too – and from belly-busting barbecue to warming biscuits and gravy, you'll find your meals served up with a mighty side of Southern hospitality.

There's also a poignant dose of history to be had here. The Civil Rights Trail takes in eighty stirring sites from Memphis' renovated National Civil Rights Museum to Birmingham, Alabama's 16th Street Baptist Church, which was bombed by white supremacists in 1963.

Aztec figurine

Teotihuacán, near Mexico City

Street food

Palacio Nacional

Making tacos

MEXICO CITY

One of the world's megacities, with more than twenty million people occupying a shallow mountain bowl at over 2400m above sea level, Mexico City has to be seen to be believed. Spreading out beyond the federal district (Distrito Federal) which is supposed to contain it, the city has a vibe which is at once edgy, laidback and cosmopolitan.

Increasingly, one of the main reasons to visit Mexico City is to eat. Full of history and culture, this Latin American metropolis features regional cuisines from every corner of the country. It is the ultimate city for street food, too. You can nibble your way through your stay at simple stalls selling traditional dishes such as tlacoyos (stuffed tortillas), tamales cooked in corn husks or a mouth-watering array of tacos, filled and topped with pork crackling, local cheese, sweet pineapple, hot chilis and exotic ingredients like nopales (cactus pads). Explore bustling food markets and dine in humble neighbourhood fondas or in classy gastronomic hot spots. Between meals, visit Mexico City's vast central square, the Zócalo, its impressive art museums and ancient Aztec ruins.

MONUMENT VALLEY

The classic southwest American landscape of stark sandstone buttes and forbidding pinnacles of rock, poking from an endless expanse of drifting red sands, is an archetypal Wild West image. Only when you arrive at Monument Valley – which straddles the Arizona–Utah state line, 40km north of Kayenta – do you realize how much your perception of the West has been shaped by this one spot. Such scenery does exist elsewhere, of course, but nowhere is it so perfectly distilled. While moviemakers have flocked here since the early days of Hollywood, the sheer majesty of the place still takes your breath away. Add the fact that it remains a stronghold of Navajo culture, and Monument Valley is one of the world's must-sees.

View from Hunts Mesa

Mural on Lower East Side

Rockfeller Center

Wall Street

Times Square

NEW YORK CITY

Cultural and financial capital of the USA, if not the world, New York City is an adrenaline-charged, history-laden place that holds immense romantic appeal for visitors. Its past is visible in the tangled lanes of Wall Street and tenements of the Lower East Side; meanwhile, towering skyscrapers serve as monuments of the modern age. Street life buzzes round the clock and shifts markedly from one area to the next. The waterfront, redeveloped in many places, and the landscaped green spaces – notably Central Park – give the city a chance to catch its breath. Iconic cultural symbols – the neon of Times Square, the sculptures at Rockefeller Center – always seem just a stone's throw away. For raw energy, dynamism and social diversity, you'd be hard-pressed to top it; simply put, there's no place quite like it.

Central Park

NIAGARA FALLS

The spectacle of water exploding over the knife-edge Niagara Falls, right on the border of the USA and Canada, is made even more impressive by the variety of methods laid on to help you get closer. Niagarans have ensured that the Falls are visible from every angle imaginable – from boats, viewing towers, helicopters, cable cars, zip lines and even tunnels in the rock face behind the cascade. At night the falls are lit up and the coloured waters tumble dramatically into the blackness, while in winter the whole scene changes as the fringes of the falls freeze to form gigantic razor-tipped icicles.

Niagara Falls comprises three distinct cataracts. The tallest are the American and Bridal Veil falls on the American side, separated by tiny Luna Island and plunging over jagged rocks in a 55m drop; the broad Horseshoe Falls, which curve their way from the USA to Canada, are far more majestic.

Horseshoe Falls

PACIFIC COAST HIGHWAY

Of all America's scenic drives, none surpasses California's Pacific Coast Highway. This spectacular route follows highways 1 and 101, running from the sunny beaches of San Diego to the redwood forests of Northern California and beyond. In 2017, Highway 1 closed for more than a year when massive landslides sent it tumbling into the sea at Big Sur. Now, after a $54 million reconstruction, you can once again enjoy this iconic drive in its entirety.

Hugging the cliffs, the road winds high above the rugged shore, giving dramatic views of white-capped surf pounding against the rocks below and sun-sprinkled waves stretching out across the horizon. There are wildlife-viewing spots, hiking trails, laidback beach towns, retro diners, seafood shacks and wineries along the way, with stops at glittering Los Angeles or hip San Francisco to break the journey. For a classic American road trip, the Pacific Coast Highway can't be beat.

The Pacific Coast Highway and the ocean below

Steller sea lion

Lumber factory near Telegraph Cove

Parliament Buildings, Victoria

Killer whale

VANCOUVER ISLAND

A rugged sliver of land cast adrift from mainland Canada, Vancouver Island may only be a ninety-minute boat journey from Vancouver, but it feels worlds apart. Its waters teem with whales, otters and dolphins, while bears and wolves roam inland – the former fishing village of Telegraph Cove is one of the best launchpads for wildlife trips. On the west coast, Pacific Rim National Park shelters a high population of black bears, which can also be seen in the Campbell River during the salmon run. There's more to this island than wildlife, though. Cowichan valley's patchwork of vineyards is an epicurean enclave, with wine tours and farm-to-table dining galore. Further south, British Columbia's capital, Victoria, sits at the island's end, with its boat-speckled marina and neo-Baroque Parliament Buildings.

Red country barn

Skiing in Stowe

Vermont welcome sign

Maple syrup

Autumn colours in Vermont

VERMONT

With its white churches and barns, covered bridges and clapboard houses, snowy woods and maple syrup, Vermont comes closer than any other New England state to fulfilling the quintessential image of small-town Yankee America. Much of the state is smothered by verdant, mountainous forests and valleys painted in a thousand shades of green; the name Vermont supposedly comes from the French *vert mont*, or green mountain.

Tourism here is largely activity-oriented, and though the state's rural charms can be enjoyed year-round, most visitors come during two well-defined seasons: to see the spectacular fall foliage in the first two weeks of October – when the green leaves of summer turn to vivid oranges, yellows and reds – and to ski in the depths of winter, when resorts such as Killington and Stowe spring to life. Vermont's fresh air and gorgeous scenery will make the soul sing.

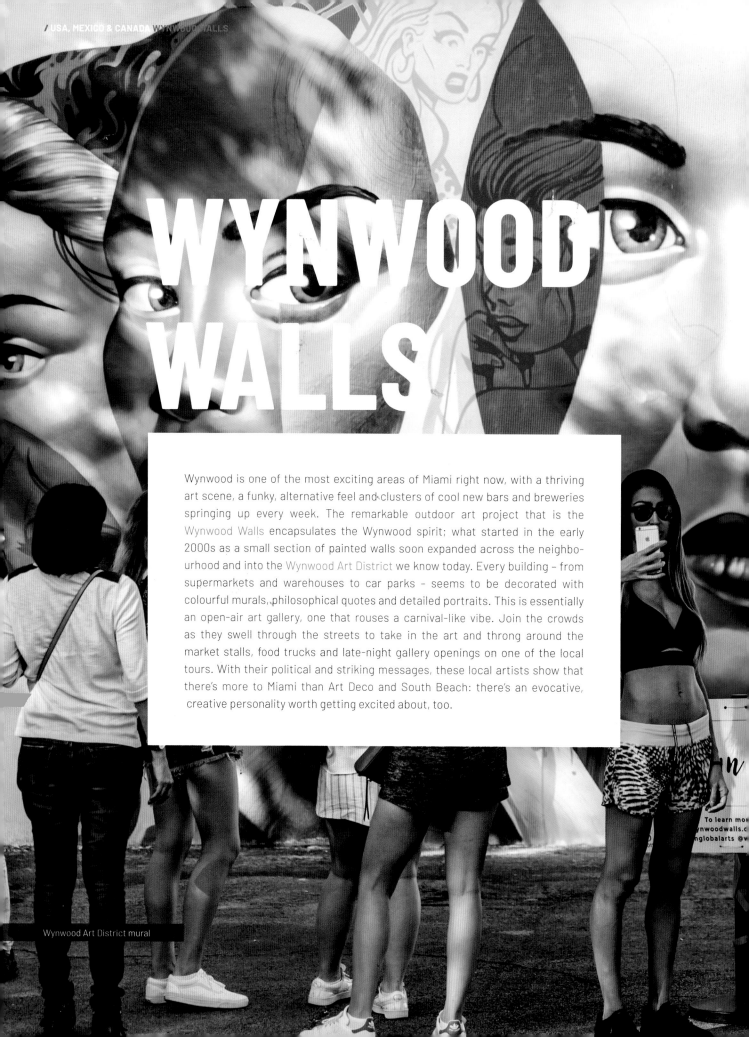

WYNWOOD WALLS

Wynwood is one of the most exciting areas of Miami right now, with a thriving art scene, a funky, alternative feel and clusters of cool new bars and breweries springing up every week. The remarkable outdoor art project that is the Wynwood Walls encapsulates the Wynwood spirit; what started in the early 2000s as a small section of painted walls soon expanded across the neighbourhood and into the Wynwood Art District we know today. Every building – from supermarkets and warehouses to car parks - seems to be decorated with colourful murals, philosophical quotes and detailed portraits. This is essentially an open-air art gallery, one that rouses a carnival-like vibe. Join the crowds as they swell through the streets to take in the art and throng around the market stalls, food trucks and late-night gallery openings on one of the local tours. With their political and striking messages, these local artists show that there's more to Miami than Art Deco and South Beach: there's an evocative, creative personality worth getting excited about, too.

Wynwood Art District mural

To learn mor
ynwoodwalls.c
nglobalarts @w

Herd of bison in Hayden Valley

YELLOWSTONE NATIONAL PARK

America's oldest and easily its most famous national park, Yellowstone National Park attracts over four million visitors every year, for good reason; the sheer diversity of what's on offer is mind-bending. Not only does Yellowstone deliver jaw-dropping mountain scenery, from the scintillating colours of the Grand Canyon of the Yellowstone to the deep-azure Yellowstone Lake and wild-flower-filled meadows, but it's jam-packed with so much wildlife you might think you've arrived at a safari park. Shambling grizzly bears, vast herds of heavy-bearded bison (buffalo) and horned elk mingle with marmots, prairie dogs, eagles, coyotes and more than a dozen elusive wolf packs on the prowl.

What really sets Yellowstone apart, however, is that this is one of the world's largest volcanoes, with thermal activity providing half the world's geysers, thousands of fumaroles jetting plumes of steam, mud pots gurgling with acid-dissolved muds and clays, and, of course, hot springs. The park might not look like a volcano, but that's because the caldera is so big – 55km by 72km – and because, thankfully, it hasn't exploded for 640,000 years.

Yellowstone Lake

Great Fountain Geyser

Grizzly bear

Majestic bull elk

CENTRAL AMERICA, SOUTH AMERICA & THE CARIBBEAN

AMAZON RAINFOREST

Explore the Amazon Rainforest and you'll find everything from poison dart frogs to snapping piranhas, spotted jaguars and ocelots, slithering anacondas and chipper monkeys, fish-eating bats and over 1300 species of bird. It's the most biodiverse place on earth and much that lies beyond the main waterway remains relatively untouched and unexplored.

This vast forest – the largest on the planet – and its giant river system cover more than half of Brazil and a large portion of South America. The forest extends into Brazil's neighbouring countries (Venezuela, Colombia, Peru and Bolivia), where the river itself begins life among thousands of different headwaters. The daily flow of the river is said to be enough to supply a city the size of New York with water for nearly ten years, and its power is such that the muddy Amazon waters stain the Atlantic a silty brown for over 200km out to sea.

The Amazon has remained virtually unchanged for the past 100 million years, for it did not pass through the same ice ages that altered other parts of the world. Some areas are still inhabited by indigenous groups who have survived through the centuries and have never had contact with the world outside their own jungle.

Bird's-eye view of the Amazon

Poison dart frog

Indigenous Desana woman

Toucan

Uyuni salt flat

Cerro Rico and Potosí

La Paz street

Baby tapir, Kaa-Iya National Park

Cordero al palo, lamb roasted above a wood fire

BOLIVIA

In recent years, Bolivia has been making the news for its high-altitude wine scene around Tarija; its Andean and Amazonian fine dining, especially in La Paz and Santa Cruz; and its long-lasting leader, Evo Morales, who's spoken out for the indigenous and mestizo masses. All of this adds to the country's appeal, but Bolivia's eternal verities and unexplored wildernesses are even more alluring reasons to make the trip.

Surrounded by Brazil, Paraguay, Argentina, Chile and Peru, Bolivia lies at the heart of South America. Stretching from the majestic icebound peaks and bleak high-altitude deserts of the Andes to the exuberant rainforests and vast savannahs of the Amazon basin, it embraces an astonishing range of landscapes and climates. In the lowlands, Kaa-Iya National Park is the place to see jaguars and tapirs, while Madidi is home to the recently discovered titi monkey; glamping is opening up these and other hitherto off-radar reserves. Up on the *altiplano*, Potosí's once silver-rich Cerro Rico mountain and beautiful Sucre offer insight into the colonial past of this former imperial powerhouse, while the Uyuni salt flat and its surrounding 4000m-high desert and snow-capped peaks will leave even the most world-weary traveller breathless.

BRITISH VIRGIN ISLANDS

Turquoise waters lap powder-soft sands as reggae beats drift from outdoor tiki bars offering fruity cocktails in true Caribbean style. Visitors to the British Virgin Islands will quickly discover the main activity here is relaxing ocean-side, sipping the juices of a coconut or a rum punch. Water-based activities – snorkelling, scuba diving or hiring a boat – are all on offer, but the islands' verdant forests may be enough to tempt sun babies away from the sandy shores. Hike up Mount Sage on the main island of Tortola for the best views, where green panoramas stretch to the azure sea and its smattering of islets and milky-white bays. Virgin Gorda also offers hiking routes through Gorda Peak National Park, as well as "the Baths" – a protected beach area where granite boulders create natural tidal pools for swimming.

Cane Garden Bay, Tortola

La Bodeguita del Medio, Havana

Street musician

Cruising down the Malecón

Che Guevara Memorial, Santa Clara

CUBA

It is difficult to be unemotional about Cuba. This Caribbean island thrills the senses, befuddles the mind and tugs at the heartstrings. It is a place full of romantic images: conga drums pounding late into the night, spicy dark rum and dazzling nightclubs, quick conversations spiked with sexual innuendo and wicked humour, people who are warm, expressive and affectionate, music emanating from every window – all enveloped within the aroma of hand-rolled cigars.

Beneath the faded grandeur of its crumbling, colonial buildings, Havana basks in nostalgia. Ride along the Malecón – its glorious sea wall – in a shiny, vintage American car. Stroll the romantic, cobbled streets of Old Havana, sipping mojitos in Hemingway bars and soaking up the Cuban beats.

Beyond the capital, there's much to explore. Learn to salsa in the beautiful colonial town of Trinidad, visit Che Guevara's resting place in Santa Clara or unwind on one of Cuba's white-sand beaches; most are still unspoilt and uncrowded. Whatever you do, a trip to Cuba is intoxicating, intriguing and unforgettable.

EASTER ISLAND

Few places have a culture quite as enigmatic as Easter Island. Despite measuring just 22 kilometres in length, it's an open-air museum on a mammoth scale. The star attractions are the 887 mysterious, monolithic *moai* statues that dot the coastline, some erected on ceremonial platforms, others abandoned in the grass. All were carved centuries ago from soft, volcanic tuff to represent and honour now long-dead ancestors.

Elsewhere, the islanders' Rapanui culture is emphatically alive. February brings the two-week smorgasbord of high-adrenaline – and perilous – events showcasing the islanders' exceptional physical prowess. During the rest of the year, watch heavily tattooed dance troupes stamping to the beat of Polynesian music in Hanga Roa's nightly performances.

Beyond the town, it's all about nature, with the peak of Volcán Terevaka granting extraordinary views of the foaming, wild ocean beyond the island's shores, while further north, tourists can linger on palm-studded, white-sand beaches.

Ahu Tongariki - the largest *ahu* on the island

View from Bartolomé Island

GALÁPAGOS ISLANDS

It's quite humbling that thirteen scarred volcanic islands and more than a hundred islets, scattered across 45,000 square kilometres of ocean, 960km adrift from the Ecuadorian mainland, should have been so instrumental in changing humanity's perception of itself. Yet it was the forbidding Galápagos Islands – known for their diverse range of species – that allowed Darwin to formulate his theory of evolution, catapulting science into the modern era. The main island, Santa Cruz, holds the Charles Darwin Research Station, where visitors can learn more about his research.

Today the archipelago's matchless wildlife, stunning scenery and unique history make it the world's premier wildlife destination. The animals that have carved out an existence on these islands have a legendary fearlessness which results in close-up encounters that are impossible anywhere else on earth. Seals sleep onshore and play in the shallow water of the harbours, giant tortoises amble along unfinished roads and marine iguanas bask in the sun on black volcanic rocks before launching themselves into the crashing waves. The waters are filled with reef sharks, turtles and swarms of reef fish, while whale sharks, hammerheads, manta rays, whales and dolphins can be spotted offshore.

Marine iguana

Resident dolphin

Charles Darwin Research Station, Santa Cruz

Giant tortoise

MACHU PICCHU

As the sun climbs above the serrated ridges of the surrounding mountains and carves its way between geometric stone plazas and palaces, you're struck by the very same magic that has enthralled visitors since this citadel was "rediscovered" in 1911. Offering one of the most substantial legacies of the Inca civilization, Machu Picchu grants unparalleled access to an empire that once stretched for 4000km.

But part of what makes this archeological site so tantalizing is the experience of getting there. For many, it's on foot along the paved, former Inca road known as the Inca Trail, or the higher-still Salkantay, which climbs giddy 4600m passes.

As tourist numbers continue to increase, those wanting to avoid the crowds should head instead to the archeological complex of Kuélap. Situated in northern Peru, 420 circular stone dwellings top a vertiginous mountain plateau and are some thousand years older than the youthful Machu Picchu.

Llama in front of Machu Picchu

NAZCA LINES

One of the great mysteries of South America, the Nazca Lines are a series of animal figures and geometric shapes, none of them repeated and some up to 200m in length, drawn across some 500 square kilometres of the bleak, stony Pampa de San José in Peru. Each one, even such complicated motifs as a spider monkey and hummingbird, is executed in a single continuous line, most created by clearing away the brush and hard stones of the plain to reveal the fine dust beneath. Theories abound as to what their purpose was – from landing strips for alien spaceships to some kind of agricultural calendar, aligned with constellations above, to help regulate the planting and harvesting of crops. More recent satellite imaging suggests the lines were connected to a sophisticated ancient aqueduct system. Regardless of why they were made, the Lines are among the strangest and most unforgettable sights in South America.

The Spiral

The Hummingbird

The Spider Monkey

The Spaceman

Basílica de la Asunción, León

Corn Island beach

Granada shop

Cerro Negro crater

NICARAGUA

While tourism booms in nearby Costa Rica and Belize, Nicaragua has remained largely under the radar. Yet this beautiful and friendly country has all the charms of its Central American neighbours – and more. It counts the second-largest rainforest in the Americas (after the Amazon) among its 78 wildlife refuges and biosphere reserves, which harbour exotic animals and brightly coloured macaws, toucans and other birds. Lovely Pacific beaches boast prime surfing spots, while the white Caribbean sands of the Corn Islands are a diving and snorkelling paradise.

Nicaragua is a land of lakes and volcanoes, with stunning landscapes everywhere you go. You can hike the volcanoes, and sandboard down lava-covered slopes at Cerro Negro. Be sure to explore the old colonial cities, too: charming Granada, with its cobbled streets and brightly painted houses, and earthy León with its magnificent cathedral and political murals.

PATAGONIA

Vast, windswept and studded with glaciers, Patagonia is a wild and wondrous landscape of the imagination. This stunning region – shared by Argentina and Chile – is home to southern right whales, orcas, elephant seals, porpoises and rich marine birdlife along its sweeping Atlantic Coast, while inland lies gold-hued steppe, big-sky country dotted with wooden estancias and solitary towns. Hiking and adventure hubs lie on either side of the Andes, all the way from Chile's lovely Lake District to end-of-the-world Ushuaia, Argentina's southernmost city. A slow road trip opens up the grandeur; alternatively, zigzagging flights reveal dazzling topographies from above.

Patagonia was christened by Portuguese explorer Ferdinand Magellan who, on making landfall at San Julián in 1520, thought the tall Tehuelche natives had unusually big feet – "pata" is Spanish for "foot". Still barely populated and celebrating its 500th birthday in 2020, Patagonia remains one of the world's most majestic, empty and awe-inspiring regions.

Patagonian Lake District

Torres del Paine National Park

Sea lions near Ushuaia

Ushuaia

RIO DE JANEIRO

The citizens of the thirteen-million-strong city of Rio de Janeiro call it the Cidade Marvilhosa – and there can't be much argument about that. Although riven by inequality, Rio has style. Its international renown is bolstered by some of the greatest landmarks in the world: the Corcovado mountain supporting the great statue of Christ the Redeemer; the rounded incline of Sugar Loaf mountain, standing at the entrance to the bay; and the famous sweeps of Copacabana and Ipanema beaches, probably the most notable lengths of sands on the planet. It's a setting enhanced annually by the frenetic sensuality of Carnaval, an explosive celebration that – for many people – sums up Rio and its citizens, the *cariocas*.

The Selarón Steps

Locals playing on Ipanema

Copacabana

Christ the Redeemer

Carnaval dancer

TAYRONA NATIONAL PARK

Giant, rounded boulders that once tumbled down steep forest-covered mountains are now battered by the tumultuous Caribbean Sea along the shores of Tayrona National Park. This wild patch on the north coast of Colombia is breached only by the occasional hiking trail, along which visitors can navigate the jungle on horseback to reach sheltered beaches like Playa del Cabo. Camping is popular here, as is swinging in hammocks, lounging by the turquoise sea, exploring the palm groves filled with giant blue butterflies and climbing over the boulders in the morning light. Of the few trails heading inland, the challenging scramble up to Pueblito, a pre-Hispanic village with no road access, is the most rewarding. Wildlife here includes more than one hundred species of mammal; look out for the spectacular, critically endangered cotton-top tamarin monkey.

Cabo San Juan del Guía

Tikal rising from the jungle

TIKAL

Towering above the rainforest, Tikal in Guatemala is possibly the most magnificent of all Maya sites. The ruins are dominated by five enormous temples, steep-sided limestone pyramids that rise to more than 60m above the forest floor. Around them are thousands of other structures, many semi-strangled by giant roots and still hidden beneath mounds of earth.

The site is surrounded by the Parque Nacional Tikal, a protected area of some 576 square kilometres on the edge of the much larger Reserva de la Biósfera Maya. The sheer scale of the place is overwhelming, and its atmosphere spellbinding. Dawn and dusk are the best times to see wildlife, when the forest canopy bursts into a frenzy of sound and activity. The air fills with the screech of toucans and the roar of howler monkeys, while flocks of parakeets wheel around the temples, and bats launch themselves into the night.

Tikal archeological site

Howler monkey, Parque Nacional Tikal

Toucan

Humpback whale

Sign encouraging conservation

Uvita's "whale tail"

Sea turtle hatchling

UVITA

Uvita is a village where beauty comes in twos. It is here – where the pristine sands of Playa Uvita meet Playa Hermosa – that the famous "whale tail", a giant sandbar shaped like a whale fin, juts into the ocean. Real humpback whales pass through twice a year during their migrations, with whale-watching trips launched from Playa Uvita; sightings are particularly common in September and October, when olive ridley and hawksbill turtles also come ashore. This stretch of Costa Rica has some of the most beautiful beaches in the country, backed by palm-speckled forest.

Costa Rica is one of the few places in the world where conservation of the natural world is a top priority. Uvita, its surrounding beaches and the tropical forest that flanks them, make up the Marino Ballena National Park, which is also home to an abundance of colourful birds, reptiles and other wildlife.

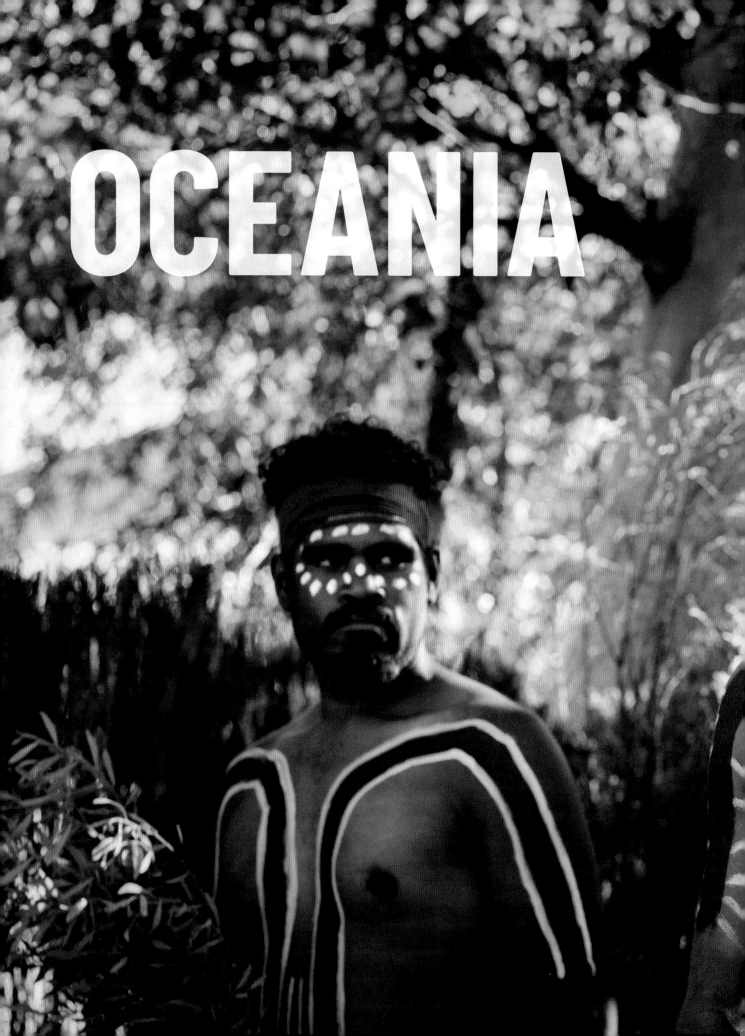

OCEANIA

FIJI

Sun-drenched beaches, turquoise lagoons, swaying palm trees – Fiji supplies all the classic images of paradise. No wonder, then, that every year thousands of travellers come to this South Pacific archipelago for the ultimate island escape. But it's not all coral reefs and cocktails: the islands boast dramatic waterfalls, lush rainforests echoing with birdsong, and remote villages where you'll find a traditional way of life continues.

While many people spend their whole time in Fiji sunbathing and sipping cocktails from coconuts, there are plenty of activities on offer, too. Within a ten-minute boat ride of most resorts you can find yourself snorkelling over colourful reefs, sometimes amid dolphins and manta rays, or scuba diving at pristine drop-offs covered in soft corals and sea fans. In addition, at the exposed edges of the reefs are some of the world's finest and most consistent surfing breaks. Further inland is a world of stunning mountains, rainforests and remote villages, where you'll find big-hearted and hospitable Fijians living a life-style similar to their tribal ancestors.

Snorkelling off Fiji

Summer hike

Walking between ice sheets

Flying over the glaciated landscape

Mountain hut, Franz Josef Glacier

FRANZ JOSEF GLACIER AND FOX GLACIER

The rugged and pristine landscape of New Zealand's South Island is the stuff of legend. Here on the west coast and just 20km apart, Franz Josef Glacier and Fox Glacier plunge from the Southern Alps almost to the sea – well below the snow line – and you can hear the grinding and cracking of compacted ice as it moves. Legend tells of the beautiful Hine Hukatere who so loved the mountains that she encouraged her lover, Tawe, to climb alongside her. He fell to his death and Hine Hukatere cried so copiously that her tears formed the glaciers, with Franz Josef known to Maori as Ka Roimata o Hine Hukatere – "The Tears of the Avalanche Girl".

Treks to Fox and Franz Josef Glacier take in the lower alpine valley to viewing areas 500m from the terminal face. But to experience the cold blue landscape up close, take a helicopter tour to the top of either glacier and explore deep crevasses, tunnels and ice caves.

Traversing Fox Glacier

GREAT BARRIER REEF

The Great Barrier Reef is to Australia what rolling savannahs and game parks are to Africa. Calling it "another world", as the commonest cliché has it, doesn't begin to describe the feeling of donning mask and fins and coming face to face with its extraordinary animals, shapes and colours. There's so little relationship to life above the surface that the distinctions one usually takes for granted – for example between animal, vegetable and mineral – seem blurred, while the respective roles of observer and observed are constantly inverted as shoals of curious fish follow the human interlopers about.

The Reef was built by one kind of animal: the tiny coral polyp. Simple organisms, related to sea anemones, polyps grow together like building blocks to create modular colonies – corals. Around their walls and canyons flows a bewildering assortment of creatures: large rays and turtles "fly" effortlessly by, fish dodge between caves and coral branches, snails sift the sand for edibles and brightly coloured nudibranchs dance above rocks.

Aerial view of the Great Barrier Reef

Dive boat at the reef

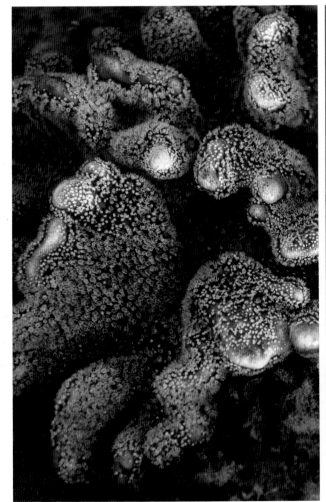

Toadstool coral

Diving with a sea turtle

Heart of Voh

New Caledonia's capital, Nouméa

Amédée Islet and lighthouse

Isle of Pines

Soursop for sale

NEW CALEDONIA

Locals gather in traditional French markets selling morning-baked baguettes, warm pastries, colourful vegetables and fresh fish in the towns of New Caledonia – a small slice of France in the Pacific Ocean. Palm-fringed beaches lie just beyond, where turquoise waters shelter a healthy abundance of bright corals and marine life. Take in the weird and wonderful creatures who call this home with snorkel and flippers or venture into the deep with full diving gear.

New Caledonia offers ecological oddities including the Isle of Pines, an island covered in columnar pines all the way to its sandy shores, and the Heart of Voh. Seen from above, it really does look like a heart – and it's all natural, created by a clearing in the dense mangroves.

The World Bar & Restaurant, Queenstown

Jetboating on the Shotover River

View over Queenstown and Lake Wakatipu

The Remarkables

QUEENSTOWN

Queenstown is the adventure capital of New Zealand, superbly set by the deep-blue Lake Wakatipu and hemmed in by craggy mountains. The thin fresh air which descends over the town is filled with the scent of pine and lingering smoke from wood fires during the winter months, when sports enthusiasts from around the globe come to ski and snowboard on the Remarkables. Queenstown has a distinctly European flavour, with its snowy peaks and the still waters of Lake Wakitipu at its centre. Locals and visitors alike gather in cosy restaurants, spilling out onto the pedestrianized streets to trade stories of fun-filled days over a cold beer or a hot chocolate.

This South Island hub hosts all manner of other adventure activities. The most prominent of these is bungee jumping, but rafting, skydiving, paragliding and jetboating are also popular. Best leave these for the summer months, however, when the temperatures have risen and the air has lost its bite.

Wild horses cooling off, Ua Huka Island

Black-tip reef sharks at the Blue Lagoon, Rangiroa

Mo'orea Island

Harpoon fishing

TUAMOTU AND MARQUESAS ISLANDS

We've all heard of Tahiti and Bora Bora with their bleach-white sands and azure seas, frequented by sun-baked celebs and love-struck honeymooners. Indeed, most visitors to French Polynesia – a collection of 118 islands and atolls in the South Pacific – will opt for one of the Society islands, but a trip to one of the less-visited archipelagos can be even more rewarding.

The Tuamotu islands are seriously off-the-grid; you won't find any shopping or nightlife options here, or even consistent wi-fi. The small coral atoll of Tikehau is particularly enchanting, with pink-sand beaches that slide into crystalline tropical waters. Fishing is still the primary money-maker here, and parts of the atoll are still virtually uninhabited. Nearby Rangiroa – one of the largest atolls in the world – is a diver's dream, with a vast lagoon (the size of Tahiti), as well as dolphins, manta rays, barracudas and sharks.

Even more secluded, the Marquesas islands are among the most remote island groups on earth, a three-hour flight from the Society islands and thousands of kilometres from the nearest continent. These raw and rugged islands are breathtakingly beautiful, with white- and black-sand beaches, looming cliffs swathed in green, and wild horses, boars and goats wandering free.

Beach on Tikehau

ULURU

If you're wondering whether all the hype is worth it, the answer is, emphatically, yes. Rising out of the parched red centre of Australia, Uluru (Ayres Rock) is the dramatic touchstone of this ancient continent. The Rock, its textures, colours and not least its elemental presence, is a sacred site to its Aboriginal custodians and without question one of the world's natural wonders.

Uluru means "meeting place", and many Aboriginal dreaming tracks or songlines intersect here. Spirituality is often grounded in more practical draws, and Uluru, with its permanent water hole, abundant animal life, shelter and firewood, has been saving lives for millennia. The rock is sacred to the local Anangu people, who resumed ownership of the lands inside the national park in 1985, in a historic handover ceremony.

Uluru

INDEX

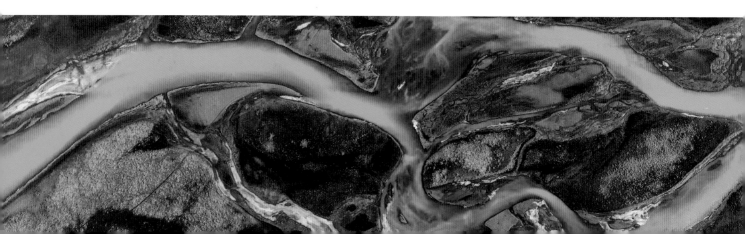

INDEX

CONTRIBUTORS

Jacqui Agate

Susie Boulton

Chris Bradley

Donna Dailey

Steph Dyson

Helen Fanthorpe

Lottie Gross

Rebecca Hallett

Tim Hannigan

Nick Inman

Jeroen van Marle

Sîan Marsh

Rachel Mills

Chris Moss

Joanna Reeves

Paul Stafford

Aimee White

PHOTO CREDITS

(Key: T-top; C-centre; B-bottom; L-left; R-right)